20 BICYCLE TOURS IN NEW HAMPSHIRE

D1378698

Wellington State Park on Newfound Lake from a viewpoint only a short walk off your route on the Canaan-Newfound Lake tour (see tour 13).

20 Bicycle Tours in New Hampshire

TOM AND SUSAN HEAVEY

New Hampshire Publishing Company   Somersworth

Acknowledgments—We want to thank Kris Sweet, Barbara Leedham, and all the friendly people in New Hampshire's towns who helped us research and write this book.

An Invitation to the Reader—Although it is unlikely that the roads you cycle on these tours will change much with time, some road signs, landmarks, and other items may. If you find that changes have occurred on these routes, please let us know so we may correct them in future editions. The authors and publisher also welcome other comments and suggestions. Address all correspondence:

Editor, *Bicycle Tours*
New Hampshire Publishing Company
Box 70
Somersworth, NH 03878

International Standard Book Number: 0-89725-001-X
Library of Congress Catalog Card Number: 78-71716
© 1979 by Tom and Susan Heavey
Published by New Hampshire Publishing Company
Somersworth, New Hampshire 03878
Printed in the United States of America

Photograph on page 2 by Nancy-Jane Jackson; pages 22-23 courtesy of the Massachusetts Department of Commerce and Development; and pages 102-103 by Ralph Morang III. All other photographs by the authors.

Cover photo by Hank Nichols

Design by David Ford

We wish to dedicate this book to our mother and friend, Barbara Leedham

N

Canada

0 5 10
miles

**20 BICYCLE TOURS
IN NEW HAMPSHIRE**

Colebrook

20

Connecticut River

Groveton

Berlin

Maine

Vermont

19
Lisbon Sugar Hill

Bartlett
18 N Conway

Orford

17
N Sandwich Tamworth

14
Hanover

13
Canaan Hebron

Connecticut River

12
Lake Sunapee New London
11

Mt Sunapee

E. Washington Henniker Hopkinton Concord
4 10
Alstead Marlow 8
Hillsboro
9

Gilsum
3 Hancock Portsmouth
Surry
Keene Francestown Exeter 16
7 Little Boars Head
Swanzey Peterborough 15 South Hampton
2 Jaffrey
1 5
Hinsdale 6 Greenville
Fitzwilliam Amesbury *Atlantic Ocean*

Massachusetts

Contents

Contents

20 BICYCLE TOURS IN NEW HAMPSHIRE

Introduction

Bicycle tours can range from half-day trips around town to marathon cross-country journeys. Bicycle touring is an activity in which nearly everyone can participate, from grandparents to youngsters. To us, bicycle touring provides an opportunity to be outside, where the air is clean and the scenery beautiful, where the terrain provides a bit of exercise and the countryside offers attractive spots for picnicking or an occasional shop for browsing. When we search for a tour—short or long, to take with our children or by ourselves—we're looking for something that will make a day memorable.

For this guide we have put together twenty tours that we hope do just that. They were selected in part to bring out New Hampshire's varied beauty from the unique vantage point of the cyclist. But beyond these criteria, we sought to identify roads that are good for biking and routes of reasonable length for the average cyclist. Whatever their reasons for pedaling, cyclists, with rare exceptions, must share the roadway with motorized vehicles. And as far as we are concerned, just any road will not do. Sharing the pavement with much larger, faster-moving vehicles operated by drivers who are often unthinking and discourteous can be more an exercise in terror and survival than a rewarding personal experience. With this book we hope we can prevent the frustration and disappointment that can come when roads are randomly selected from maps.

Selecting a Tour

These loop tours have been developed from our experience with The Biking Expedition operating bicycling trips for both adults and teenagers since 1973. They range in length from fourteen miles to over one hundred miles and in difficulty from easy to challenging. Particular attention in the tour descriptions has been given to the sorts of information necessary for you to decide which trips you are capable of and will enjoy. We have attempted to remove unpleasant surprises, but not the adventure!

The tours are organized in the book roughly geographically, starting with an easy pastoral ride in the state's southwestern corner and ending with a grand trip around Coos County, north of the White Mountains. All are loops, ending where they start. At the beginning of each tour we summarize the tour distance, trip difficulty, and terrain characteristics. From this information, you should be able to decide whether a particular trip appeals to you. If it does, read on to obtain specific directions and information about points of interest, places to purchase food, and road conditions, all of which are necessary for a safe, organized, and enjoyable tour. Note that each tour direction is preceded by a cumulative mileage figure (the distance you have traveled to that point). Information about points of interest, food availability, and road conditions follows the specific tour direction.

We would like to point out that our evaluation of road conditions is not based on scientific study of road characteristics but upon our personal experience as cyclists. Five criteria are used in judging the suitability of a road for biking: apparent volume of traffic, width, presence of paved shoulders, visibility or sight distance, and condition of pavement. To us, low traffic volume is the most important factor for safe cycling; consequently, in setting up trips we attempted to keep you off major roads and on backcountry roads. While these rural lanes tend to be narrow and sometimes bumpy, lack shoulders, and have limited visibility, they usually carry very little traffic and are therefore safer. There are times when we had no choice but to use more heavily traveled routes. In these cases we point out the hazard and advise special caution—or urge you to save the route for off-season times when the volume of traffic is usually lower.

Can you do it? It may seem like a silly question to some, but to many, the thought of pedaling a bicycle for twelve, twenty, or more miles is a fearful challenge. The prospect of having a mechanical problem with the bike, or being on some deserted rural road in state of complete exhaustion, of climbing long and painfully steep hills, of having a sore backside from that hard, narrow seat—all loom like giant roadblocks in front of many aspiring cyclists. While we do not advise the uninitiated to bite off more than they can chew, most of these fears soon disappear if you use common sense and take reasonable precautions. If you have questions about your capabilities, start with the shorter tours on less hilly terrain.

Preparing for a Tour

As in all sports, there are a few things in bicycle touring that can make the difference between a happy, fulfilling experience and a disappointing one. Before you begin touring, you should know something about bicycle touring equipment, bicycle maintenance, your physical condition, and bicycle safety.

Equipment. In general, we recommend a ten-speed bicycle for touring in New Hampshire, although a five-speed is certainly acceptable for trips in the easy and moderate categories. Unfortunately, single-speed and three-speed bikes do not offer the gear range necessary to conquer New Hampshire's inevitable hills. On the other hand, the five- and ten-speed derailleur bicycles afford tremendous mechanical advantage; once you learn to shift them efficiently so you maintain an even cadence, major barriers to both speed and hill climbing disappear. With a five- or ten-speed, most anyone can ride six miles per hour without strain, and given reasonable health and some practice, most adults can average ten to fifteen miles an hour (racing cyclists can do twenty or more miles per hour!).

For touring, a ten-speed bicycle should weigh thirty pounds or less, have good quality center pull or side pull brakes, and have a gear ratio low enough to allow for hill climbing. In the simplest terms possible, this means having twenty-six to thirty-one teeth on the largest sprocket on your freewheel and thirty-six to forty teeth on your smaller chainwheel. We also find that narrow seats, down-turned handlebars, and toe clips all help improve cycling efficiency, but these are not essential equipment for touring.

The kind of equipment you have does make a difference and, as with most sporting gear, you get what you pay for. In the world of bicycles, quality is generally synonymous with strong, light-weight frames; high-quality, precision-manufactured components; and careful assembly. So beware of discount specials. Today there are many moderately priced bicycles available that will perform very well on all the tours described in this book. Information about the various makes and models—and on riding techniques—is available in many publications.

Bicycle Tools and Emergency Repairs. For even a half-day tour, you should know how to make simple repairs to your bicycle.

You don't need to be an experienced mechanic to make some of the more basic repairs to your bicycle.

Probably the most common breakdown cyclists encounter is a flat tire. To repair it, you should have a patch kit to fix the tube, tire irons to remove the tire from the rim, and a pump to inflate the tire after the repair. If you bring along a spare tube as well, you won't have to patch the punctured one during the trip—unless you get a second flat tire. Another breakdown you should be prepared to deal with is a broken derailleur or brake cable. While this repair is not difficult, it is more time consuming and requires more tools. You need a third hand (this is the name for a tool) to hold the brakes closed, appropriate sized wrenches to loosen the nuts on the brakes or derailleur, and a pair of needle-nose pliers capable of cutting wire, since most universal brake cables have different sized nipples at either end to accommodate two types of brakes. One of the nipples has to be cut in order to thread the cable. Finally, derailleur adjustments generally require a small phillips head or narrow-headed screwdriver. You should also consider carrying a small metric tool kit and an eight-inch adjustable wrench.

In addition to the tools and spare parts mentioned, we suggest you pack the following for longer trips: a freewheel tool that fits your freewheel cluster, a chain rivet remover, a spoke wrench, spare spokes that fit your wheel, a cotterless crank tool if you have a cotterless crank or cotter pins if you have a cottered crank, spare brake blocks, a roll of electrical tape, a few spare nuts and bolts, a small can of lubricating oil, a tube of grease, and cone wrenches.

Volumes have been written about bicycle repairs and maintenance, and we urge you to purchase a small pocket-sized book to take with you if you are at all uncertain about your ability to repair your bike. Most adjustments are not difficult, even for those whose maintenance know-how normally stops with light bulb replacement. As with many other endeavors, fear of the unknown can be a major block to new experiences.

Physical Condition. Your physical condition is important to consider before taking up cycling. Obviously people vary widely when it comes to cardio-vascular efficiency, and the potential for over-extending yourself exists in cycling to the same degree that it does in other sports. Fortunately cycling, like walking, jogging, or cross-country skiing, is primarily an individual activity—one you can and should undertake at your own pace. There is little excuse for over-extending yourself, and you have only yourself to blame if you give in to the temptation to do too much too soon. Of course, if you have been physically inactive for a long period or are over thirty-five, it is probably a good idea to have a thorough physical before you begin touring. But one of the major advantages of cycling is that it is an activity in which you can participate throughout life. In addition, if proper gearing techniques are used, it is usually easier on your knees and feet than jogging is .It also has the benefit of offering the kind of moderate sustained physical involvement that helps improve cardio-vascular efficiency.

Safety. Cycling is a safe and fun activity, if you adhere to certain principles and rules of safety. One of the major problems with bicycling is that cyclists are permitted to use roadways without first obtaining a license, or otherwise demonstrating knowledge concerning the proper operation of a bicycle and rules of the road. Although New Hampshire statutes state all cyclists are "subject to and must follow all rules and regulations applicable to the operator of a motor vehicle except those rules that, by their nature, have no application," in practice anyone can ride a bicycle almost anywhere or any way he or she wants. No appointed group or organization is responsible for teaching bicycle safety, and it generally receives a low priority from enforcement agencies , with the result that people can and do ride as they please. It is little wonder, then, that accidents involving bikes are not uncommon.

But it does not have to be that way, especially if you adhere to the following guidelines: BE ALERT, BE VISIBLE, and BE PREDICT-ABLE. You must be ALERT because you cannot depend upon a motorist to look out for your welfare; you must be ready to take evasive action if necessary. Common examples of this type of situation include: a motorist making a right turn after passing a cyclist causing the cyclist to ride into the side of the turning vehicle; a motorist making a left turn at an intersection into the path of an oncoming cyclist; and a motorist in a parked vehicle opening a door into the path of the oncoming cyclist or pulling out from a parking place without yielding to the cyclist.

You must be VISIBLE in order to give the motorist every

opportunity to see you. Most drivers are courteous if they see you, but they are not generally looking for cyclists. Rather, they are looking for other cars and trucks, which pose more personal danger to them than do cyclists. It should come as no surprise that, according to a recent study, a large percentage of fatal cycling accidents occur at night when visibility is reduced. Three things a cyclist can do to enhance visibility are to wear bright clothing, use bicycle flags, and NEVER ride at night.

Your movements on your bicycle should be PREDICTABLE. Many bicycle accidents occur when cyclists make sudden turns or move into the path of a vehicle without allowing the driver sufficient time to take evasive action. Examples of such situations include: a cyclist riding from a midblock location into traffic; a cyclist riding into cross traffic from an intersection controlled by a stop sign or traffic signal; and a cyclist riding along the right side of a street and then suddenly veering left into the path of a car.

In addition to being alert, visible, and predictable, there are some other specific actions you can take to protect yourself while cycling. The most important is to WEAR A HELMET. Your head is the most vulnerable part of your body, and a good quality helmet, such as the Bell Helmet or the MSR, can make the difference should you fall. Another important precaution is to stay in control on downgrades. It is easy to forget that a bicycle can reach speeds of forty-five to fifty-five miles per hour on steep downgrades. At those speeds, it does not take a very large obstacle such as a rock, pothole, or patch of sand to throw you out of control.

Finally, a few common sense bike riding rules are: ride in a straight line, never zigzag; ride in single file, always with traffic, never against it; listen for approaching traffic that you may not yet see; keep enough space between you and the bike in front of you to allow for an emergency stop; be alert for road hazards such as potholes, loose gravel and sand, parallel storm grates, expansion joints on bridges, and especially railroad crossings, where tracks can easily throw you out of control. And always practice defensive cycling.

Remember, on the tours outlined in this book you are often on backcountry New Hampshire roads where the scenery is beautiful and the traffic very light. In such settings, it is easy to be lulled into a sense of security and safety. But always be alert for an unexpected vehicle coming over the top of the hill or around the next bend, because the driver is probably not expecting you either.

Cycling is fun, healthful, and refreshing. Get involved, and may you have a long hill down and a stiff tailwind!

Monadnock Region

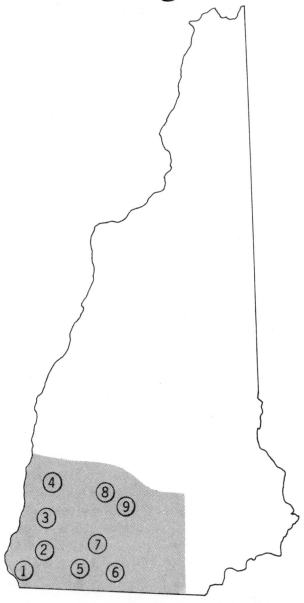

1

Tri-Stater

25.8 miles; easy to moderate cycling
Level to rolling terrain

While this is a book about bicycle touring in New Hampshire, in the interest of safety and good touring, we have bent the ground rules somewhat for this loop through the fertile farmland of the Connecticut River Valley. Our Tri-Stater starts in the southwestern part of the Granite State, crosses into Northfield, Massachusetts, and winds back though Vernon and Brattleboro, Vermont. If you have successfully completed one of the easy, half-day trips or wish to impress your friends with your superb physical and athletic ability by cycling three states in one day, this is the trip for you. Actually, it is a great trip for anyone who can appreciate the majestic beauty of the Connecticut River and the serenity of country roads that twist and wind to open up new scenes around every bend.

The tour begins at a wayside rest area on NH 119, about 1 mile south of the Hinsdale Raceway. Developed by Boy Scout Troop 307 in a shady pine grove next to the Connecticut River, it offers sufficient room to park your car.

0.0   From the rest area, head east on NH 119 toward the center of Hinsdale for 2.7 miles to NH 63, on your right.

On your way into Hinsdale you pass several other small wayside picnic areas with great views of the Connecticut River.

Several food stores line the stretch of NH 119 between the rest area and the raceway. There are also several drive-in restaurants and food stores on NH 119 just beyond the NH 63 junction, as well as in the center of Hinsdale.

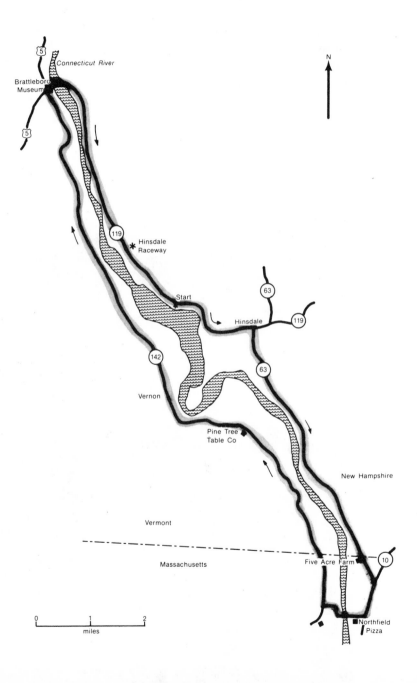

NH 119 in this area has a good surface but no shoulder except for a .4-mile section at the trip's beginning. The terrain here is rolling with several short, moderately steep upgrades. Traffic is generally light to moderate.

2.7 Turn right onto NH 63 and ride south for 5.5 miles. You cross the state border into Northfield, Massachusetts, just before reaching MA 10.

Many productive, working farms dot the rolling countryside of the Connecticut River Valley.

A great road for cycling, NH 63 twists, dips, and turns as it hugs the eastern edge of the Connecticut River Valley. High enough to provide long views of corn fields and grazing cattle, yet without mind-blowing hills to challenge your legs and heart, it is a delight to ride. Two small picnic areas on the right, one 1.6 miles and the other 3.2 miles from the NH 119/NH 63 junction, offer nice spots to bask in the scenery. Five Acre Farm, located .5 mile before you reach MA 10, sells fresh vegetables during the summer. Pauchaug Brook Fish and Wildlife Management Area, operated by the

Massachusetts Division of Fisheries and Wildlife, is located at the junction of the two highways.

NH 63 is narrow with no shoulders but a smooth surface. Visibility is generally good except at an occasional sharp turn or sudden dip. Traffic tends to be light.

8.2   At the intersection, turn right onto MA 10/MA 63 and ride .6 mile to an unmarked road on the right, just before the Northfield Pizza House.

Northfield–Mount Hermon School, a coeducational boarding school, is set high above the Connecticut River adjacent to MA 10/MA 63 on the northeast side of Northfield.

In addition to the Pizza House, there are several stores and restaurants in Northfield on MA 10/MA 63 south of our turnoff.

MA 10/MA 63 is a wide, two-lane road with a smooth surface. While it is a major route with some truck traffic, this short section that leads into town is generally safe to travel because the speed limit is low.

8.8   By the Northfield Pizza House, turn right onto the unmarked road, and prepare yourself for a rapid, twisting descent to a bridge over the Connecticut River. After crossing the river, the road makes a sharp right and then a sharp left over a railroad bridge before meeting VT 142, 1.6 miles from MA 10/MA 63.

If you turn left (south) when you reach VT 142 and ride for .1 mile, you come to a general store.

Initially, the unmarked road VT 142 is narrow, steep, and twisting and requires caution. However, on the west side of the river it is quite level with good visibility.

10.4   At the intersection, turn right and head north on VT 142 for 11.2 miles to VT 119 in Brattleboro.

Much like NH 63 on the other side of the Connecticut River, this route offers easy cycling through prosperous farm country with occasional views of the river. Pine Tree Table Company's factory store, located on the left in 3.4 miles, is open seven days a week. Two historical markers, one for Vernon's First Meeting House and the other for the tomb of Jemima Tute (1723–1805), famed "fair captive," are located at 4.3 miles and 6.2 miles respectively. The Brattleboro Museum and Art Center, located at the junction of VT 142 and US 5 in Brattleboro is open Tuesday through Sunday from 1:00 p.m. to 4:00 p.m.

Brattleboro is a large enough town to support many restaurants and food stores.

VT 142 is a smooth, narrow, two-lane road with no shoulder and light traffic. Visibility is generally good except for a few areas where curves and grades limit sight distance. For the most part the terrain is quite flat, though there are a few rolling hills. You should be alert for several railroad crossings, especially near Brattleboro.

21.6 At the intersection, turn right toward New Hampshire, head down a short hill (beware of the railroad tracks at the bottom!), and cross the Connecticut River (be careful on the slippery iron grate bridge). As you cross, the road becomes NH 119. Continue for 4.2 miles to your car—and a soft seat.

NH 119 is a wide road with good visibility. The shoulder, of variable width and poor quality, is of little use to the cyclist. Traffic is generally light to moderate except during racing times at Hinsdale Raceway, when it can be heavy. There is one short, steep hill to climb soon after you cross the bridge over the Connecticut.

25.8 You made it! You are back at the rest area where you began your trip.

2

Swanzey Covered Bridges

17.2 miles; easy cycling
Level to rolling terrain

Covered bridges are as characteristic of New Hampshire as maple syrup, baked beans, and church suppers. Their presence yields a comforting sense of permanence and continuity with the past, as well as a release from the plastic and glitter of twentieth-century life. Swanzey, in the southwest corner of the state, is proud possessor of four such spans, all conveniently connected by a network of gently rolling country roads. On this route, an excellent beginning trip for both adults and children, you experience a kinship with early farmers and settlers, who like you, traveled these byways over the same bridges in nonmotorized fashion.

When you reach these relics, take a moment to examine how they are put together. Because covered bridges were originally built to carry loaded haywagons over rivers and thus were designed and constructed by local farmers, each has its own character. The roof and siding that cover the bridge (which had to be high enough to accommodate the loaded wagons) were meant primarily to safeguard the truss work, not passersby, from the elements.

A convenient starting point for this trip is at the junction of NH 32 and Sawyers Crossing Road, in the center of Swanzey. Monadnock Regional High School and Swanzey Town Hall, both adjacent to this intersection, have parking lots where you can leave your car.

0.0   From the high school or town hall in Swanzey, head south on NH 32 for 1.5 miles to Carlton Road.

The Bunthaus, on the right side of NH 32 a short distance south of Monadnock Regional High School, features doll arrangements, a miniature house, and hand-carved copies of antique furniture. It is open between 9:00 a.m. and 5:00 p.m., Tuesday through Saturday from the beginning of July to the middle of October.

NH 32 is a two-lane road with no shoulder, a smooth surface, good visibility, and low traffic. The terrain is mostly level.

1.5 At Carlton Road, turn left and travel 1.1 miles, passing through your first covered bridge, to an unmarked crossroad (note the B.G. Curry Real Estate office in a white, twin-chimney colonial on the left at this intersection).

The Carlton covered bridge, which spans South Brook, is thought to be one of the oldest covered bridges in the area. It is constructed

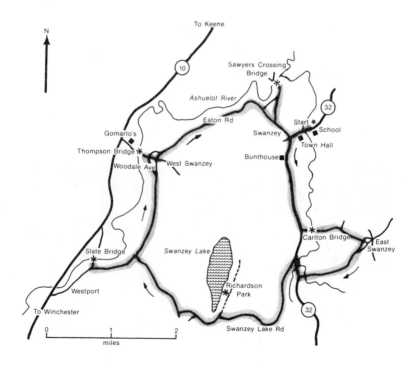

in the Queenpost truss style, a design used on the earliest bridges that farmers built employing the same methods they used for their churches and barns. Although once quite common, few bridges that were constructed in this style are standing today.

Carlton Road is quite level, except for one moderate upgrade just beyond the bridge. It is narrow and has no shoulder, little traffic, and an acceptable surface for cycling.

2.6   By the B.G. Curry Real Estate office, turn right to head downhill past the East Swanzey Post Office, and then bear right as you merge with another unmarked road. A biker's delight with a smooth, level surface, this road brings you back to NH 32 in 1 mile.

The back roads in this area are all much alike. They tend to be narrow with no shoulder, have reasonably smooth surfaces with

The Thompson Bridge still has one of its two sidewalks.

occasional frost heaves, and pass over slightly rolling terrain.

3.6 At the intersection, bear right on NH 32, riding north for .2 mile to Swanzey Lake Road, on the left.

3.8 Turn left onto Swanzey Lake Road, which you follow for 3.9 miles to a T-junction with an unmarked road.

If you are looking for a place to go swimming, bear right off Swanzey Lake Road onto the dirt road that rings Swanzey Lake. In about .3 mile you'll come to Richardson Park, which offers swimming and picnicking for a $1 admission charge.

Swanzey Lake Road is similar to the other backcountry roads you travel on this tour. It has a number of twists and turns, but if you stay on the surfaced road, you should not get lost.

7.7 At the T-junction, turn left, heading toward Westport and Winchester (beware of railroad tracks a short distance along this road), and ride .7 mile to a stop sign.

8.4 At the stop sign, turn right toward Keene, and ride .1 mile to the Slate covered bridge.

The Slate covered bridge stretches 142½ feet across the Ashuelot River. Built in 1862, this bridge replaced another that had been erected in the same spot in 1800.

8.5 Retrace your route to the T-junction with Swanzey Lake Road and continue straight for another 1.7 miles to a stop sign in West Swanzey.

11.0 At the stop sign, turn left onto Woodale Avenue, so that you cross the railroad tracks and pass Holbrook Homes Boarding House. Shortly, you come to a crossroad, where you turn left again, and .2 mile from the stop sign you reach the Thompson covered bridge.

This bridge, which also spans the Ashuelot River, originally had two sidewalks and still has one today.

For refreshments, stop at Gomarlo's Inc., on the west side of the Thompson covered bridge. This store is open all day, every day.

11.2 Retrace your route to Woodale Avenue, and bear left. Keeping right at the fork, follow this road to Eaton Road. Here bear left again toward Swanzey Center. In 2.4 miles you reach Sawyers Crossing Road.

13.8 Turn left onto Sawyers Crossing Road and ride 1.5 miles to the last and longest covered bridge on this tour.

The Sawyers Crossing covered bridge, like the Thompson and Slate bridges, is an example of Town lattice truss construction. This type of covered bridge design was developed in the early 1830s by Ithiel Town, a great engineer of his time.

15.3 Retrace your route to the intersection with Eaton Road and turn left to continue on Sawyers Crossing Road for .4 mile back to your start.

17.2 You are at the intersection of NH 32 and Sawyers Crossing Road, where you began the tour.

3

Surry Mountain–Gilsum

**22.3 miles; moderate to challenging cycling
Rolling to hilly terrain, one major hill**

Because it offers lots of variety, our trip around Surry Mountain, just north of Keene, can be approached in a number of ways. It is ideal for cyclists who seek the solitude of an early morning ride along the Ashuelot River, the challenge of a steep hill near Gilsum, and the exhilaration of a long descent to the city of Keene. Those who wish a full day's outing have their choice of any number of activities to break up the cycling: a stop in Keene, an active college town, is the perfect counterpoint to a trip through the countryside; the Surry Mountain Recreation Area, whose dam and reservoir were built as a flood-control project by the Army Corps of Engineers in 1941, offers outdoor activities from swimming to camping; and Gilsum, the site of some sixty inactive mines which a century ago produced beryl, rose quartz, and even gold, is an enticing detour. Bears Den Geological State Park, with its huge boulders and large "potholes," and Ashuelot Gorge are both also worth a visit, especially for those interested in unusual geologic formations.

The trip begins at Surry Mountain Recreation Area on NH 12A, 5.5 miles north of Central Square in Keene. Do not follow Dam Road, which leads to the dam and office building. Continue 1.1 miles past this road to the entrance of the day-use area, on the right, where a large parking lot, changing house, beach, picnic tables, and well-maintained grounds are located. The parking lot can be used from the beginning of May until the end of September only; it is flooded during the remaining months.

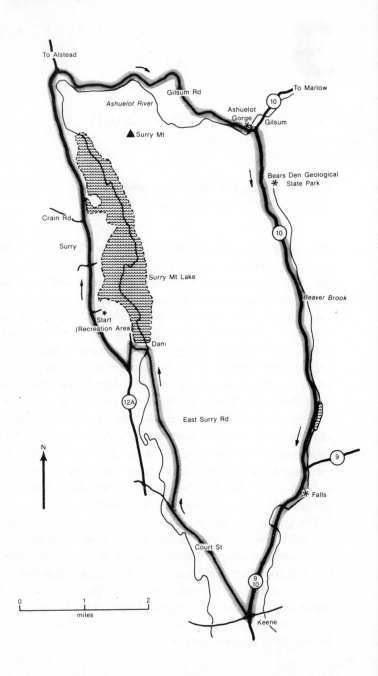

0.0   From the parking lot, return to NH 12A and turn right, heading north for 3.8 miles to Gilsum Road, on your right.

Surry Mountain Recreation Area offers swimming, boating, hiking, picnicking, fishing, and camping. The village of Surry is located 1.1 miles north of the recreation area entrance, off NH 12A on Crain Road.

NH 12A has a smooth surface and good visibility, but no shoulder. The terrain is flat to rolling. Traffic tends to be light but picks up during commuting hours.

3.8   Turn right onto Gilsum Road and proceed for 4.2 miles to NH 10.

Here you wind alongside the Ashuelot River through a small valley where the vegetation varies from thick forest to open meadow. Ashuelot Gorge, at the junction of Gilsum Road and NH 10, is worth a look from the stone arch bridge that spans it. If you turn left on NH 10 and ride toward Gilsum, you can take advantage of a swimming area to your left on the Ashuelot River. Should you wish to explore old mines or dig for semi-precious stones, stop at the Gilsum Village Store or write to the Gilsum Library (Box 57, Gilsum, NH 03448) for a copy of an area map ($.25). Or, for a fee of $1.00, you can dig in a mine owned by Francis Maloney, who runs the Village Gem Shop in the center of Gilsum. The mine is located several miles from the village and the ride there includes about .3 mile of dirt road. If your timing is right, you can attend Gilsum's annual Rock Swap, held during the last week of June. During the Swap, hundreds of rockhounds trade, dig, and buy various types of semi-precious stones.

The two-lane Gilsum Road is narrow, with no shoulder and a moderately bumpy surface. Because of its many twists and turns, visibility is limited; however, traffic is light. The terrain is moderately hilly, with a very gradual rise as you proceed upstream along the Ashuelot. A steep .3-mile downgrade with a sharp turn awaits you 3 miles after turning on Gilsum Road. Caution is advised.

8.0   Turn right onto NH 10 and immediately begin a steep .8-mile climb, the trip's most difficult, and continue for a total of 5.3 miles to the junction of NH 10 and NH 9.

From a bicycle you have an opportunity to enjoy many scenes which often escape the motorist.

Bears Den Geological State Park, whose entrance is on NH 10 at the top of the .8-mile-long grade, is a mountainside covered with gigantic boulders and large "potholes" of unknown origin. As it is easy to lose your footing, local officials urge caution when walking through the area.

NH 10, a major north/south highway, has a smooth surface, adequate width, and generally good visibility. There is an intermittent shoulder of variable width and generally poor quality. With the exception of the steep hill immediately south of Gilsum Road, the terrain is either level or slopes down towards Keene. There are some trucks, but except for peak periods on weekends, traffic conditions are usually acceptable. While this road is not generally recommended for young children or very inexperienced cyclists, most people should have no major difficulty here.

13.3   At the junction of NH 10 and NH 9, bear right onto NH 9/NH 10 and ride 2.6 miles to Central Square in Keene.

On the left .3 mile beyond this junction there is a wayside rest area with a lovely waterfall, a nice spot to relax or picnic.

At this writing the junction of NH 10 and NH 9 was undergoing major reconstruction and so may be altered by the date of publication. This stretch of highway is much like that you just rode; however, the speed limit is substantially lower as you enter Keene, and traffic usually slows down.

15.9   When you reach Keene, proceed approximately one-quarter of the way around Central Square, turn sharply right onto Court Street near the Keene Food Mart, and continue on Court Street for 2.1 miles to East Surry Road (note the sign for Bretwood Golf Course).

Many fine colonial and Victorian homes line the streets around Central Square. Keene State College, Thorne Art Gallery, and Wyman Tavern are but a few of the many attractions in this community.

There are numerous restaurants and food stores in Keene, among them the Keene Food Mart directly on your route here.

Court Street has moderate to heavy traffic. For .8 mile, its wide shoulder is also used for parking, so be alert for people opening car doors in your path. The road is reasonably flat, and a sidewalk exists all the way to East Surry Road.

18.0   At East Surry Road, bear right and ride for 2.8 miles to Dam Road.

East Surry Road has a smooth surface, no shoulder, and low traffic. Note that the road makes a sharp left turn and goes over a small bridge beyond the golf course. Just stay on the paved road.

20.8   At Dam Road, turn left and ride for .4 mile to NH 12A.

Dam Road also has a smooth surface, no shoulder, and little traffic.

21.2   At the junction with NH 12A, turn right and cycle 1.1 miles back to the Surry Mountain Recreation Area.

22.3   You are at the entrance to the day-use area and the end of your trip.

4

Alstead–Marlow

25.1 miles; challenging cycling
Level to hilly terrain

Alstead, Marlow, and South Acworth: vintage New Hampshire at its best! Here there are no resorts or suburban developments, only tree-shaded lanes along mountain brooks that tumble and roll on their way to the Connecticut River and individualists whose spirit and fortitude are infectious. Here you sense that life is neither hurried nor complicated. While some bicycle tours should be approached as an experience in solitude, this is not one of those; the residents of these towns seem more than willing to share themselves and their experiences with you, and you should enjoy them. A retired printer turned rockhound, a seventy-five-year-old proprietor of a general store, and a young cabinet maker who always has a pot of coffee on the stove: these are the people who can make this trip more than just a day's ride.

Because you are touring rugged land that rises upward and eastward from the Connecticut River Valley, this tour is not particularly easy. In fact, fully one-third of the route, about eight miles, involves a climb, some of it steep. But the other two-thirds is either flat or downhill. It's not a bad ratio, especially as you do the climbing early in the trip. Your efforts are rewarded by outstanding scenery and about sixteen miles of effortless biking.

The tour begins in the village of Alstead, located on NH 12A/NH 123, approximately twenty-five miles north of Keene. Main Street, which is the numbered highway, offers ample opportunity for on-street parking. There is also space at the Shedd Porter Memorial

Library at the village's west end; however, we suggest that you check with the librarian before parking there.

0.0   Begin by traveling east on Main Street (NH 12A/NH 123) past the stores and school for .7 mile to the junction with NH 123A.

     The Village Store, on Alstead's Main Street, is the only place to buy food until you reach NH 10 in Marlow, about ten miles into your tour. NH 12A/NH 123 has a smooth surface, two wide lanes, very little shoulder, and light to moderate traffic.

0.7   At the junction, take the right fork and continue on NH 12A/NH 123 toward Keene for another .7 mile, where the road forks again.

1.4   At the fork, stay left on NH 123 where NH 12A heads south to Keene. Continue on this road through Mill Hollow and East Alstead for 8.3 miles to NH 10 in Marlow.

     This stretch offers numerous views of farmland set against

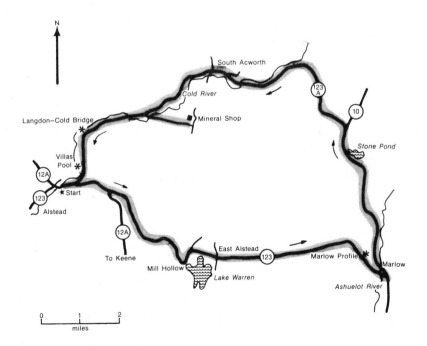

mountains. Mill Hollow, a late-eighteenth-century community of small, individually operated mills, still has a standing grist mill. East Alstead is a hilltop town with well-kept homes and a fantastic view of Lake Warren to the southwest. Four miles beyond East Alstead you pass beneath the Marlow Profile, a rocky cliff that bears a close resemblance to New Hampshire's symbol of the Great Stone Face.

After NH 12A splits off toward Keene, NH 123 narrows and the shoulder disappears completely. However, the visibility is good and there is little traffic. You climb nearly the entire 8.3 miles to Marlow. For the most part the slope is gradual, but there are occasional steep pitches, which are sometimes relieved by a level stretch or downgrade.

9.7 At the junction of NH 123 and NH 10 in Marlow, turn left on NH 10 and ride north for 4.5 miles to NH 123A, on your left.

In the center of Marlow, named after famed playwright and author Christopher Marlowe, the grounds around a lily pond offer a pleasant rest stop. The Ashuelot River and Stone Pond are located along your route.

The Marlow Grocery is located on NH 10.

NH 10 provides a smooth surface for biking. While it has only an intermittent shoulder and moderate traffic, including some trucks, the visibility is good and the terrain quite flat, resulting in easy, enjoyable cycling.

14.2 At the junction, turn left and follow NH 123A for 10.2 miles downhill through South Acworth to NH 12A/NH 123, back in Alstead.

The Cold River, a shallow, rocky stream paralleling the road, offers frequent opportunities for a refreshing wade. Harvey Bailey's Beryl Mountain Mineral Shop is located 1 mile off your route but is well worth the extra 2 miles cycling to visit. Watch for a sign saying "Mineral Shop" on a bridge to your left 2.4 miles beyond the tiny hamlet of South Acworth. The sign is easy to miss, so for reference look for a barn and farmhouse across the road from the bridge. The sign points left to an unmarked road, which you follow 1 mile over a smooth surface and flat terrain to the shop. Open "eight days a week," it contains a large collection of mica, rose quartz, garnet, pyrite, and other minerals collected from abandoned mines in the area. However beautiful the stones, it is really the genial Mr. Bailey who makes the trip worthwhile. A retired printer, he freely shares his extensive knowledge of the history and location of New Hampshire mineral sites with anyone who asks.

Beyond the cutoff to the mineral shop you pass the Langdon–Cold River covered bridge, a seventy-eight-foot span built in 1869 by Albert Granger. Just before you reach NH 12A/NH 123 again you

The Cold River and its quiet undisturbed banks offer a refreshing rest stop on the Alstead-Marlow tour.

coast past Villas Pool, a popular swimming and picnic area that offers swan boat rides in the summer.

In South Acworth the Village Store, founded in 1865, is open Monday through Saturday from 7:00 a.m. to 6:00 p.m. and Sunday from noon to 4:00 p.m. If you do stop, take a moment to visit the Gehan Family Pottery shop located behind the grocery store. The Gehan Family offer for sale many one-of-a-kind pottery pieces.

The first 2.1 miles on NH 123A descend steeply alongside a tree-shaded brook. On a sunny day the lacy shadows make it difficult to see the bumps and cracks in the road. Be forewarned that the road turns sharply left at the bottom of this steep stretch. The remaining miles to Alstead slope less steeply downward. The road is narrow and winding and has a rough but very ridable surface. There is no shoulder.

24.4   At the junction turn left onto NH 12A/NH 123 to retrace the last .7 mile to the village of Alstead.

25.1   You are back where you started.

If you have time, continue past the library and over the bridge to the Alstead Village Cabinetmaker. Donald Pecora, the young proprietor, may treat you to a cup of coffee as he demonstrates how he handcrafts the toys and furniture for which he has gained a considerable reputation.

5

Jaffrey-Fitzwilliam

20.2 miles; moderate cycling
Rolling terrain, some short, steep hills

Mount Monadnock, rising nearly 2,000 feet above surrounding hills to a peak of 3,165 feet, is the most dominant land feature in southwestern New Hampshire. Tucked in its shadow are the towns of Jaffrey and Fitzwilliam, whose rolling terrain and secondary roads offer fine opportunities for bicycle touring. Since this tour is relatively short and only moderately demanding, it can easily be combined with stops at historic sites and antique shops or a side trip up Mount Monadnock if you have a full day to spend in the area.

Begin your trip in Jaffrey at the junction of US 202, NH 137, and NH 124. Ample parking can be found along the main street and in the municipal parking lot.

0.0 From Jaffrey, head west on NH 124 for 5.2 miles through Jaffrey Center to Fitzwilliam Road, on your left. There's a red farmhouse on your right at this turn.

The Jaffrey Civic Center on the right side of NH 124 just west of the US 202/NH 137 junction, is the place to pick up information about the area's points of interest and learn about its fascinating history and people. They include Willa Cather, the Pulitzer-prize-winning writer who is buried in Jaffrey Center; Amos Fortune, a negro slave who purchased his freedom in Massachusetts at the age of fifty-nine and then moved to Jaffrey in 1781 where he established a tannery and lived as a highly respected citizen until his death in 1801; and Hannah Davis, a spinster left destitute at the age of thirty-four who supported herself by manufacturing wooden hat boxes, which have since become collector's items. The Civic Center is open every Saturday afternoon from 1:30 to 5:00 (603-532-6527 or 532-8811). In Jaffrey Center, which you pass through in 1.6 miles, there are several historic homes and buildings, including the Old Meeting House, First Church, Amos Fortune's grave, and The Little Red Schoolhouse.

If you would like to learn a bit about the area's natural history, watch for the signs to Monadnock State Park .5 mile beyond Jaffrey Center. The road leads 2 miles into the park to Monadnock Ecocenter, an education and information center operated by the Society for the Protection of New Hampshire Forests at the trailhead of the White Dot Trail up the famous mountain.

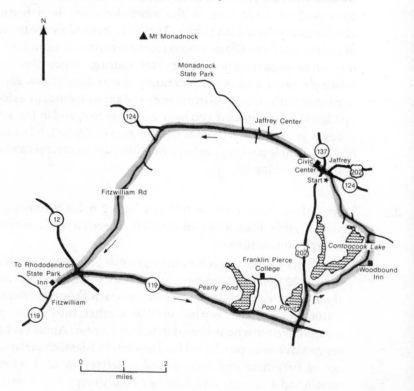

There are several stores and restaurants in Jaffrey, the last place to buy food until you reach Fitzwilliam.

From Jaffrey to Jaffrey Center, NH 124 has a smooth surface and a two-foot-wide paved shoulder. Visibility is good, the terrain gentle, and the traffic moderate. As you leave Jaffrey Center, the road narrows and the shoulder disappears. The surface remains smooth, though.

5.2 At Fitzwilliam Road, bear left. Stay left at the fork .6 mile from NH 124, and continue another 2.9 miles, mostly downhill, to NH 12.

Fitzwilliam Road is a narrow backcountry road with a reasonably smooth surface, no shoulder, good visibility, and very little traffic.

8.7 At the intersection, turn left onto NH 12 and then almost immediately right onto NH 119 to ride into Fitzwilliam. Follow NH 119 a short distance to the village green, circle it, and then retrace your route to the junction of NH 12 and NH 119.

In Fitzwilliam there are a number of antique shops worth visiting. The Fitzwilliam Inn on the common has been offering passersby lodging, food, and good cheer since 1796. The Meeting House and Blake House, two more historical buildings on the green, are also worth noting. For a side trip, you may wish to ride 2.6 miles northwest of the Fitzwilliam green to Rhododendron State Park. Encompassing sixteen acres of wild rhododendrons, it's one of the largest tracts of this species north of the Allegheny Mountains. While your efforts as a cyclist to reach the park are hindered by a bumpy, hilly road, it is well worth a visit in mid-July when the blossoms are at their peak.

Roy's Market is on NH 119 just before the Fitzwilliam green. The Fitzwilliam Inn serves lunch from noon to 2:00 p.m. and dinner from 6:00 p.m. to 9:30 p.m. daily. The Fitzwilliam Hearth, at the junction of NH 12 and NH 119, serves lunch from 11:30 a.m. to 2:30 p.m. and dinner from 6:00 p.m. to 9:30 p.m., Monday through Saturday.

NH 12 and NH 119 through Fitzwilliam are narrow, with moderately heavy but slow-moving traffic.

9.5   From the junction, proceed east toward West Rindge along NH 119 for 5.6 miles to the junction with US 202.

Franklin Pierce College, on your left 4 miles east of Fitzwilliam, is a four-year, liberal arts school that was founded in 1962. It enrolls over seven hundred students.

There is a general store at the junction of NH 119 and US 202 in West Rindge.

NH 119, here wide with a good surface but no shoulder, leads you over rolling terrain. It generally carries moderately heavy traffic, but the visibility is excellent.

15.1   At West Rindge, turn left onto US 202 and follow it north 1.2 miles

If you maintain an even cadence, the rolling terrain on this tour should present no problem.

past Poole Pond (on your left) to an unmarked road on your right just beyond a sign for Woodmere Campground.

US 202 is wider than NH 119 and has paved a shoulder eight feet wide that is suitable for biking. While US 202 is a major route, its wide shoulder and excellent visibility make it very safe for cycling.

16.3 Beyond the sign for the campground, turn right onto the unmarked road and follow it for .3 mile.

Once you leave US 202, the roads back to Jaffrey are all typical rural New Hampshire lanes. Winding over rolling terrain, they have bumpy surfaces, no shoulders, and only fair visibility, but what little traffic they carry travels slowly.

16.6 At the fork, turn sharply left and continue 2.3 miles past the golf course and the Woodbound Inn to a stop sign at a T-junction.

The Woodbound Inn, a forty-room inn/resort on Contoocook Lake just outside the Jaffrey town line, offers a wide variety of summer and winter sports, including a par three golf course which is open to the public.

18.9 At the stop sign, bear left past the beach, stay left at the fork just beyond, and .3 mile from the stop sign, bear right where an unmarked road comes in from the left. Jaffrey is now only 1 mile away.

The beach on Contoocook Lake is maintained by the town of Jaffery and is open to the public.

20.2 You are back on NH 124 in Jaffrey, where you began this trip.

6

Greenville–New Ipswich

28.6 miles; challenging cycling
Hilly terrain

The southern New Hampshire towns of Greenville, Temple, and New Ipswich contrast the ways in which economic growth developed in the state during the nineteenth century. Although they are neighboring towns, each has its own distinctive characteristics.

Greenville was an early mill town that grew up in the 1800s when the agricultural industry began to falter and the manufacture of textiles was introduced to this area along the Souhegan River. The textile industry spread and flourished throughout the state of New Hampshire until the 1930s, when most companies moved to southern states. Many of the abandoned red brick mills lining Greenville's main street had been ignored until recently when restoration was undertaken for current uses as a public library, an inn, and a restaurant, among others.

The other side of nineteenth-century life in the New England of the industrial revolution is represented in the vintage homes of New Ipswich. Its fine white buildings, most notably Barrett House, are authentic and very representative of that era. Near Greenville and New Ipswich lies the tiny hilltop town of Temple, whose Grange Hall testifies to the dominance of agriculture in its past.

These three towns are connected by a network of secondary roads with light traffic and pleasant views. Since there are a number of hills to conquer on the way, this tour is suggested as an all-day trip for those who can accept the challenge of some steep hills to earn the rewards of long downgrades.

The tour begins at the south end of Greenville at the junction of NH 123 and NH 45. Leave your car along Mill Street (NH 45), which offers ample parking.

0.0   From the junction, proceed north on Mill Street for .4 mile, where NH 45 makes a ninety-degree turn to the left up a steep hill.

The red brick mill structures of Greenville and the old railroad station, which has been converted into the Depot Restaurant, provide a vivid picture of nineteenth-century industrial life.

There are several grocery stores in the center of Greenville, and, of course, you can dine in the Depot Restaurant.

NH 45 is quite narrow as it climbs out of Greenville. However, it runs through a residential area and the traffic generally travels slowly.

0.4   At the turn, follow the numbered highway .7 mile uphill and then another 3.4 miles to the town of Temple.

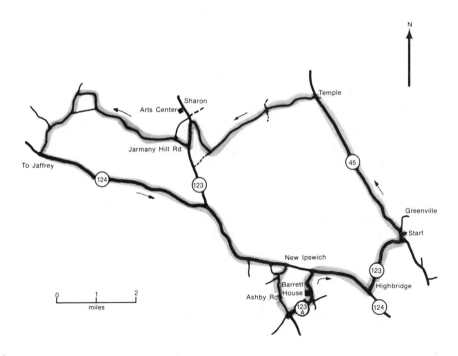

A visit to Barrett House is an appropriate change of pace for the touring cyclist.

From the top of the hill on NH 45 north of Greenville center you are treated to a fine view of the surrounding mountains.

At the top of the hill, NH 45 widens and the pavement is smooth, although the shoulder is bumpy. Traffic is generally light.

4.5 Just before you reach the cluster of buildings in the center of Temple, turn left onto the unnumbered road to Sharon. Ride for 1.6 miles, where the paved road forks and a dirt road enters from the far right.

In Temple you can buy food at the IGA store that you can see a short distance beyond the turnoff to Sharon.

From Temple to Sharon the roads are typical of backcountry New Hampshire: narrow, winding, hilly, with overhanging trees, no shoulders, frost heaves, and very little traffic.

6.1 At the fork, bear right on the paved road and continue 1.8 miles to the next paved road on the right.

7.9 At this intersection, turn right onto the paved road and cycle for .4 mile to another junction.

8.3   At this intersection, bear right again and ride .6 mile downhill to the junction of NH 123.

Across NH 123 and just to your left is the Sharon Arts Center, which displays and sells works of art and crafts created by New Hampshire artisans. Its art gallery is open to the public free of charge from May to December. The League of New Hampshire Craftsmen Shop is also open during those months. Classes are conducted throughout the year.

8.9   From the intersection, head south on NH 123 for .8 mile to Jarmany Hill Road.

NH 123 is a two-lane road with a smooth surface, no shoulder, and moderate traffic.

9.7   At this intersection turn right, downhill, to follow Jarmany Hill Road 3.5 miles to a yield sign.

Jarmany Hill Road is a winding, narrow country road. Because traffic is very light, it is ideal for biking.

13.2   From the yield sign, bear left and proceed for 1 mile to a brown house at the foot of a hill, where the road forks. Bear left up a short hill on the hard-packed gravel road and ride .9 mile to NH 124.

The hard-packed gravel should present no problem if you cycle with caution.

15.1   Turn left onto NH 124, which merges with NH 123 in 4.5 miles, and continue a total of 7.3 miles to Dark Lane Road, to your right on the outskirts of New Ipswich. Watch for a large building with brown-stained siding on your right at this intersection.

NH 124 is a fairly level, smooth, two-lane road with moderate traffic. For the first mile, its shoulder is gravel, but the roadway then widens with a paved shoulder suitable for cycling. After merging with NH 123, the road climbs for .7 mile before leveling off again. Over this uphill stretch the highway is narrow and the paved shoulder disappears, so caution is urged. Beyond the hill, the road again has a decent shoulder.

22.4   Turn right onto Dark Lane Road, riding uphill for .5 mile to Ashby Road.

Dark Lane Road is a narrow, lightly traveled country lane.

22.9   Turn left onto Ashby Road and follow it downhill for 1 mile through
        pretty surroundings—birch trees, stone walls, and attractive old
        homes—to NH 123A.

        There's an excellent view of the mountains to the north just as you
        turn onto Ashby Road. Further along, there is Appleton Manor
        Farm, a well-landscaped horse farm with a winding gas-lit drive-
        way, white-fenced paddocks, and barns.

23.9   At the intersection with NH 123A, turn left to follow the numbered
        route 1.5 miles through New Ipswich, where you rejoin NH 123/NH
        124.

        Take some time to enjoy the fine old buildings lining the road into
        New Ipswich: the Congregational Church, Town Hall (1817),
        Friendship Manor, Parsonage, and Barrett House, a Federal-style
        mansion built shortly after 1800 and furnished with exceptionally
        fine period pieces. It is open to the public from June to October,
        Tuesday through Saturday, between 11:00 a.m. and 5:00 p.m.
        There is a $1 admission charge.

        Food is available at Phil's Market on NH 123A in New Ipswich.

        NH 123A is a narrow, winding road through a residential area, but
        that should not present a problem, since most traffic obeys the low
        speed limit.

25.4   At the intersection with NH 123/NH 124, turn right and ride 1.5
        miles to Highbridge, where the two numbered routes split again.

        You can purchase snacks and drinks at New Ipswich Market on
        NH 123/NH 124.

        NH 123/NH 124 is again a smooth-surfaced road with a good
        shoulder and moderate traffic.

26.9   In Highbridge, turn left onto NH 123 and ride 1.7 miles back to
        Greenville through rolling countryside along the Souhegan River.

        NH 123 has no shoulder, a fair surface, and little traffic.

28.6   You are back at your starting point in Greenville.

7

Hancock–Peterborough

17.4 miles; easy to moderate cycling
Rolling terrain, several hills

Hancock, named for the man who was president of the Continental Congress, a signer of the Declaration of Independence, and the first post-Revolutionary governor of Massachusetts, does not flaunt its history or its charm. Yet, in its quiet way, the town does convey a vivid sense of the past. Known for its most typical old New England Main Street, it brings together in one place all the scattered pieces of an illusive picture of nineteenth-century life: picket fences, a bandstand on the green, the wood frame school, a meeting house and an inn, and stately old homes. But here the past has been adapted to modern-day life; Hancock does not seem contrived or too perfect. The John Hancock Inn, in operation since 1789, still caters to hungry and tired travelers, and the 1788 Meeting House, whose bell was forged in Paul Revere's foundry, functions today as it did two hundred years ago. The town's Museum of Antiques reinforces these ties with earlier times.

Off the beaten track some eight miles north of Peterborough, Hancock is easy to reach via US 202 and then NH 123 West. Parking does not present a problem as there is usually space along Main Street (NH 123) or by the white clapboard elementary school, where cars can be left for a few hours.

0.0   From the bandstand on the green, take NH 137 south down a steep hill to Middle Road, on the left shortly after the road levels. There is a sign for Sargent Camp at this junction.

In addition to the points of interest already mentioned, look for the Hancock Toy Shop, also on Main Street, where children's furniture and wooden toys are made.

A general store on Main Street in Hancock is the last place to buy food until you reach Peterborough.

NH 137 is narrow with a smooth surface, no shoulder, and light traffic.

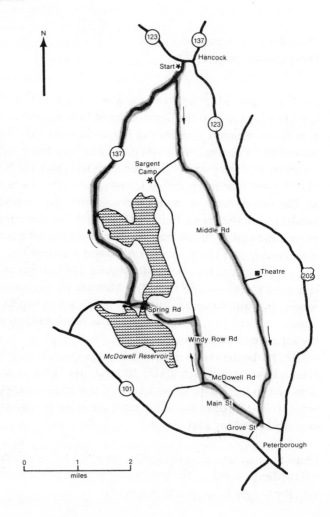

0.3   By the sign for Sargent Camp, turn left and follow Middle Road, which runs through a mixture of nicely maintained old farms and homes interspersed with woods, for 7.2 miles to Main Street in Peterborough.

Approximately 1.5 miles from the junction of Middle Road and NH 137, note the sign and right turn for Sargent Camp, a year-round outdoor education center operated by Boston University. It is open to the public (there is a charge) and offers hiking, fishing, swimming, overnight lodging, and meals. For information or reservations, call 603-525-3311. At 4.1 miles, a left turn leads to the Peterborough Players summer stock theatre. No matinees are offered, but an evening performance is an excellent way to cap a delightful day's bike tour. Reservations are advised (603-924-7585).

Like NH 137, Middle Road is narrow and carries little traffic. The road surface is not as smooth as NH 137, however. The terrain here is rolling to hilly, with one gradual climb nearly a mile long and several short descents.

7.5   At the intersection, turn right onto Peterborough's Main Street, head up a short steep hill, and continue for 1.8 miles, past the Peterborough playground, to Windy Row Road, on the right.

Eastern Mountain Sports (EMS) and Hancock Village Outfitters, two large outdoor equipment retailers, are located in Peterborough. EMS can be reached by turning left at Main Street instead of right and then left again onto US 202. The store is on the right, 2.7 miles from Main Street. Hancock Village Outfitters is on Grove Street, the street on your left immediately after you turn right on Main Street. The store is on the left in .4 mile. There is also a town park on Grove Street, to the right, with picnic tables and shade trees. The Peterborough Historical Society, also on Grove Street, has collections and displays open to the public every afternoon Monday through Friday during the summer.

Peterborough, a town of 4,500, has numerous food stores and restaurants. There are no stores on your return route to Hancock, so stop here if you wish something to eat.

Main Street in Peterborough is wide with a good surface but a rough shoulder. Traffic is moderate to heavy, since you are in a densely populated area. Except for one short, steep grade as you go up Main Street, the terrain is not difficult.

9.3   From Main Street, turn right onto Windy Row Road and begin a gradual climb past several lovely homes and farms with great views of Pack Monadnock Mountain to the east. In 1.2 miles, just beyond Anandale Farm, you come to Spring Road, on your left.

The McDowell Colony, a center for writers, painters, and musicians, is located on McDowell Road, off Windy Row Road. While not generally open to the public, this retreat has hosted many famous people, among them Thornton Wilder, who is thought to have written "Our Town" while in residence here.

Nicely maintained old farms interspersed with woods characterize much of the Hancock-Peterborough tour.

Windy Row Road has a fair surface with some frost heaves and no shoulder. Traffic tends to be light.

10.5   At the junction with Spring Road, turn left and ride 1.3 miles to NH 137.

The Game Preserve on Spring Road is a mini-museum that displays more than seven hundred early American board and card games.

Spring Road also has a fair surface with some frost heaves and no shoulder. The way to NH 137 is mostly downhill.

11.8   At the junction with NH 137, turn right and follow the numbered route 5.6 miles back to Hancock.

NH 137 is narrow and winding with no shoulder but a good surface. The terrain is rolling and visibility is limited, but traffic is generally light. There is a twisting downgrade for 1.4 miles just before you reach the intersection with Middle Road where you turned off earlier. Because trees along this stretch cast shadows on the roadway, it is often difficult to read the surface accurately. Consequently, caution is advised on this descent.

17.4   You are back at your start by the bandstand in Hancock.

Pierce Homestead–Hillsboro Center

19.8 miles; moderate cycling
Rolling to hilly terrain, several hills

Lovewell Mountain, the fourth highest peak in southern New Hampshire, provides a graceful backdrop for this Currier and Ives tour. But perhaps the most enticing aspect of the trip is the absence of commercial tourism. You can wind unhurriedly along lightly traveled byways and become enveloped by the constantly changing landscape around you—dairy farms with open pasture, thick forests, restored homes set in rural quietude, and small villages with long histories. While recommended as an all-day tour for flower-pickers and picnic-lovers, this trip can be completed in a half-day spurt by those bent on improving their cardio-vascular systems.

The recommended starting point is the Franklin Pierce Homestead near the intersection of NH 9 and NH 31, three miles west of Hillsboro. A polite request for permission to park generally results in an affirmative reply from the manager.

0.0   From the Franklin Pierce Homestead, travel north on NH 31 for 1.9 miles to a fork in the road. Just before the fork there is a dark brown house with attached barn and a signpost for East Washington on the right.

The Franklin Pierce Homestead is the family home of the fourteenth president of the United States. The house, which is tastefully decorated and furnished with period antiques, is open between 9:00 a.m. and 5:00 p.m., except Mondays, from mid-June to Labor Day. Admission is $.50 for adults and free for children under ten. The Village Gallery further north on NH 31 sells plants and local crafts.

The Corner Store at the intersection of NH 9 and NH 31 is open daily. William's General Store, 1 mile north on NH 31 is open daily, with shorter hours on Sundays (8:00 a.m. to 1:00 p.m.). This is the last store until Hillsboro, sixteen miles away.

NH 31, with the exception of the first mile which has recently been reconstructed, is rolling, narrow, and has no shoulder. The road surface is old and rough but quite ridable. Traffic is generally light.

1.9   At the fork, turn right toward East Washington and continue for 3.3 miles to a T-junction. This section of road is known as Coolidge Road

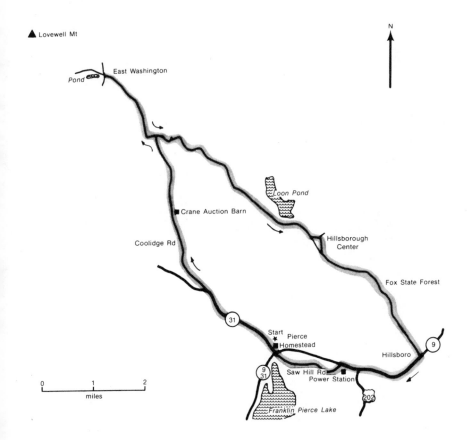

on town maps; however there are no signposts indicating this.

At Lachut's Farm you can watch prize Holsteins grazing. Several antique shops along the way welcome browsers. Country auctions are held frequently at Crane's Auction Barn.

Coolidge Road is narrow but generally has a fair surface. The terrain is rolling for about 2 miles followed by one long downgrade.

5.2 At the T-junction, turn left and ride 2 miles through a scenic valley to the village of East Washington.

Many of the uncongested country roads in the Hillsboro area are ideal for family biking.

The village of East Washington, with towering Lovewell Mountain mirrored in its calm pond, impresses the traveler with its quiet serenity.

The two-mile stretch through the valley has no shoulder and many frost heaves, but, on the positive side, very little traffic.

7.2   From the pond in East Washington, retrace your route for 2 miles to the T-junction. Proceed straight for 4 miles to Hillsboro Center.

Hillsboro Center is a small, picturesque community and historic district. Among its early churches and houses stands the 1773 homestead of its first minister. Although these buildings are not open to the public, their antiquity makes them of interest to the passerby.

This is a narrow country road with a cracked and bumpy surface. Again, very light traffic provides freedom for the cyclist. After 1.8 miles the road begins a gradual rise that continues for 2.2 miles to Hillsboro Center. The last .3 mile is very steep.

13.2   From Hillsboro Center, continue on the same road for 3.5 miles more to the junction of NH 9 in the town of Hillsboro.

Fox State Forest, a game refuge and forestry research center, is laced with a network of hiking trails. The open farmland below Hillsboro Center offers some spectacular views of the mountains of southern New Hampshire.

This stretch of road is somewhat wider and smoother than the previous one, although it should still be considered very much secondary. This is all downgrade, the longest coast of the day. Traffic is light.

16.7   In Hillsboro, turn right and ride 1.7 miles on NH 9 to a paved road by a brick power station at the base of a long hill. Both the power station and paved road are on the left.

Since Hillsboro is the commercial center of the surrounding towns, a number of stores and restaurants provide food and drink.

NH 9 is a major east-west route and consequently is the only section of the tour that does not provide pleasant cycling. While the speed limit is low, traffic can be moderate to heavy, and the shoulder is inadequate for cycling.

18.4   By the power station, turn left onto the unmarked paved road (Saw
Hill Road) and follow it for 1.4 miles to the intersection of NH 9 and
NH 31.

Saw Hill Road is a return to narrow, bumpy road conditions with
very little traffic.

19.8   You are back at the Franklin Pierce Homestead at the junction of
NH 9 and NH 31.

Crotched Mountain–Colby Hill

The distance, difficulty, and terrain are stated at the beginning of each day's directions.

Bicycling is an activity easily adapted to personal tastes, desires, and attitudes. With possibilities ranging from an evening ride around the block to an extended cross-country tour, only the imagination limits how the simple, efficient, nonpolluting bicycle can be used as a source of recreation and adventure. For variety, try coupling an active day of cycling with an overnight stay in the warm, inviting atmosphere of an old New England inn. They are found in the various nooks and crannies of New Hampshire, and each has a character all its own molded by the personalities of many generations of innkeepers an l the weathering of New England seasons. You should expect th.: floors to slant and the stairs to creak, for these are signs cf respectability and endearment, a form of homage to an elder statesman. And after a day of riding, a hot bath, a home-cooked dinner, and a warm bed, you feel like you have come to visit with a 1 old friend in the country.

Two inns conveying such warmth and friendliness are the Crotched Mountain Inn in Francestown and the Colby Hill Inn in Henniker. Conveniently accessible to each other by bicycle, they are joined by a network of roads through small towns and appealing countryside. We have designed this trip for the weekend cyclist who seeks to combine a healthy dose of moderate exercise with the warm atmosphere of a friendly home.

We suggest you start at the Crotched Mountain Inn, located adjacent to Crotched Mountain Ski Area, off NH 47, 3.6 miles north of Francestown. The Inn is an old rambling brick and wood colonial, which was recently converted into its present use. With a spectacular view of southern New Hampshire from the lawn, it sets the perfect tone for your two-day trip. Call ahead for reservations (603-588-6841), and then plan to arrive in the afternoon or early evening in time to enjoy the tennis courts and pool. The innkeepers, John and Rose Perry, go out of their way to provide you with an enjoyable stay.

The Colby Hill Inn is a lovely colonial house built around 1800. The congenial members of the Glover family are both the proprietors and hosts at the inn. They offer elegant yet comfortable accommodations and dining for their guests and the public (dinner is served every day but Monday). For reservations for your overnight stay call 603-428-3281.

Day One

21.6 miles; moderate cycling
Rolling terrain

0.0   Begin your tour from the Crotched Mountain Inn by riding 1 mile back to NH 47.

1.0   When you reach NH 47, turn left and ride for 5.2 miles to Bennington.

A number of antique shops along this route invite browsing. In this part of southern New Hampshire you ride through picture-postcard villages and countryside.

NH 47 is a narrow, winding road with a smooth surface, light traffic, and no shoulder. Because you are heading away from Crotched Mountain, the land generally slopes downward, making cycling easy.

6.2   At the junction of NH 31 and NH 47 in Bennington, turn right onto NH 31. Almost immediately, NH 31 turns left to take you along the Contoocook River, past the Monadnock Paper Mill, to the junction of US 202.

There is a grocery store in Bennington, should you need to purchase food.

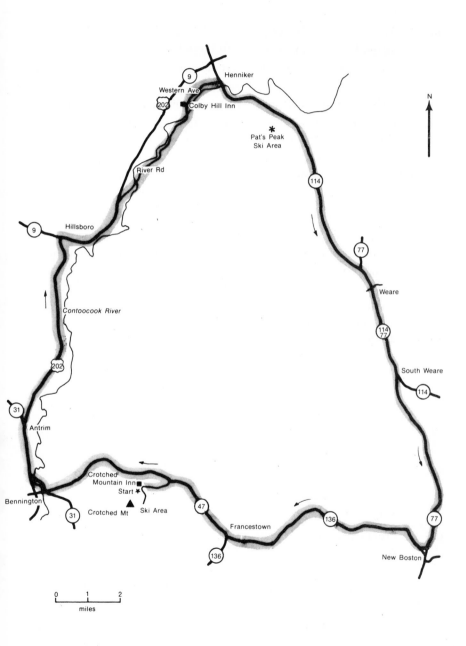

Henniker

9
Western Ave
202
Colby Hill Inn

*
Pat's Peak
Ski Area

River Rd

114

9
Hillsboro

77

Weare

114
77

Contoocook River

South Weare

202

114

31

Antrim

77

Crotched
Mountain Inn
Start

136

Bennington

31   Crotched Mt   Ski Area

47

136

Francestown

New Boston

136

N

0   1   2
miles

6.8   At the junction, turn right onto US 202/NH 31 and ride for 1.6 miles through Antrim, where the numbered highways split.

Groceries are available at a food store in Antrim.

US 202, a major route, has a smooth surface, an intermittent shoulder, good visibility, and generally light to moderate traffic.

8.4   When the numbered highways divide, bear right on US 202 and ride 6 miles to Hillsboro, where US 202 joins NH 9.

About 1.5 miles beyond Antrim you reach a section of US 202 with a wide paved shoulder, which continues for 3.3 miles.

14.4   At the junction in Hillsboro, turn right onto US 202/NH 9 and ride for 3.1 miles through town to River Road, on the right.

Food is also available in Hillsboro.

The section of US 202/NH 9 through Hillsboro has no shoulder and moderate to heavy traffic, especially on weekends. However, the speed limit is low and the visibility is good. Just as you reach what is obviously new pavement, you come to your turn by River Road.

17.5   At the intersection of River Road, by the sign for West Henniker, turn right and cycle for 4.1 miles to Colby Hill Inn, on your left.

River Road has a smooth surface, no shoulder, many curves, and several short, steep hills. Because it parallels the Contoocook River downstream, the riding is generally easy.

21.6   You are at Colby Hill Inn, your destination on Day One of this tour.

Day Two

28.1 miles; moderate cycling
Rolling terrain

0.0   From Colby Hill Inn, continue along River Road, now called Western Avenue, .5 mile to the center of Henniker.

Henniker is home to New England College, a small, experimental liberal arts school with thirteen hundred students; Pat's Peak, a popular regional ski area; and the Pole and Pedal, a sport shop specializing in bicycles, cross-country skis, and outdoor equipment.

This group of tourers prepares to start out from the Colby Hill Inn in Henniker, one of New Hampshire's many fine country inns.

There are both food stores and restaurants in Henniker.

0.5 In Henniker, turn right onto NH 114 and continue for 11 miles to the junction of NH 114 and NH 77 in South Weare.

You can purchase food at restaurants and groceries in Weare, which you pass through on your way to South Weare. There is also a general store in South Weare.

NH 114 is rolling to hilly, with downgrades in your favor. The shoulder varies from one that is wide and paved, suitable for biking, to nothing at all. Visibility is generally very good except for the.2-mile stretch just before the center of Weare. There, the road curves over hilly terrain, and we urge caution. While traffic is normally light to moderate, some large trucks do use this route.

11.5 In South Weare, turn right onto NH 77 toward New Boston. In 5.7 miles, just as you come into the village, you intersect NH 136.

You can purchase food at the general store in New Boston.

NH 77 has a good surface but very little shoulder. Normally traffic is light. The terrain is rolling, generally in your favor.

17.2   At the junction in New Boston, turn right onto NH 136 and ride for 7.3 miles to Francestown.

One-half mile before the center of Francestown you pass a historical marker describing a nearby quarry that once yielded high-quality soapstone.

There is a general store in Francestown.

When you turn onto NH 136, you begin a gradual climb that continues all the way back to the Crotched Mountain Inn. It should not present a problem to most cyclists, however. This route is rather curvy with no shoulder and very little traffic.

24.5   In Francestown, turn right onto NH 47 and cycle 2.6 miles back to the road to the Crotched Mountain Ski Area and the inn.

27.1   At the road to the ski area and the inn, turn left to cycle the last mile of your tour.

28.1   You are back at the Crotched Mountain Inn, where you began your two-day tour.

Dartmouth-Lake Sunapee Region

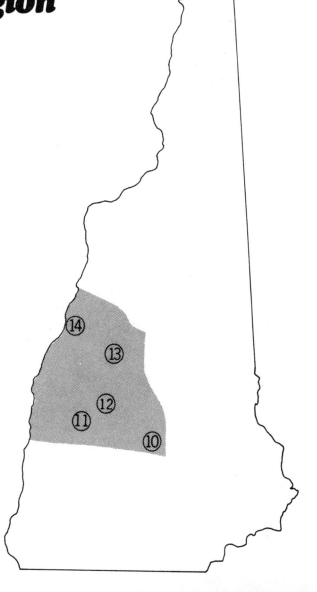

10

Concord–Hopkinton

14.1 miles; easy cycling
Level to rolling terrain, with several short hills

Offering an excellent introduction to the world of cycle touring, our Concord–Hopkinton trip couples easy biking along little traveled roads with convenient access to New Hampshire's capitol. In fact, although about half the tour is within Concord's city limits, the roads you travel there take you past several ponds and farms as well as the campus of St. Paul's School. Just over fourteen miles long, the tour is ideal for a morning or afternoon jaunt and is particularly suited for introducing the family to bicycle touring. You are also treated to the pleasure of a traffic-free ride along a bicycle path which parallels I-89 for 1.4 miles. Built at the same time as I-89, it was constructed to provide access for bicyclists, pedestrians, and St. Paul's students to Turkey Pond, which was cut off from the campus when the highway was built. The path also functions as a convenient connector between a network of lightly traveled rural roads.

We suggest you start adjacent to Exit 3 (Stickney Hill Road) of I-89, approximately four miles northwest of the intersection of I-89 and I-93 south of Concord. A short access road on the south side of I-89 leads left off Stickney Hill Road to a bicycle path. Park along the side of this access road and begin your trip.

0.0 After the exit ramp from I-89, Stickney Hill Road turns into a bumpy, two-lane byway (the only road in the area so it's difficult to get lost). Follow this paved road west as it twists and turns for 3 miles to its intersection with Jewett Road.

While there are no specific points of interest along this rural section, you pass several attractive farms and homes.

From the end of the bike path to Jewett Road, the Stickney Hill Road is narrow and bumpy but nearly free of traffic. Much of it is shaded by a tunnel of trees, offering cool cycling on hot summer days. With the exception of one upgrade as you begin your trip, the terrain is not hilly.

3.0　　Turn right at Jewett Road and ride .6 mile, over the interstate, to US 202/NH 9/NH 103.

Boulder Farm Vegetable Stand, located at the intersection of US 202/NH 9/NH 103 and Jewett Road, is good for stocking up on fresh produce during the summertime.

3.6　　Turn left and ride for 1.1 miles through the center of Hopkinton to the general store, The Cracker Barrel, at the west end of town. Here NH 103 diverges to the right from US 202/NH 9 toward Contoocook.

The main street of Hopkinton is well worth a meandering visit to view the beautiful colonials, large white churches, and impressive town hall, all set back from a roadway lined with magnificent shade trees. St. Andrew's Church on the village common, built in 1827–1828 and designed by architect John Leach, is of Granite Ashlar

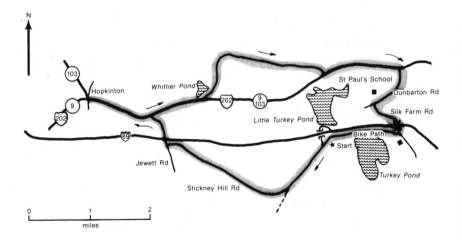

construction, a style typical of New England Episcopal churches in the period.

The Cracker Barrel sells groceries and other miscellaneous items.

US 202/NH 9/NH 103 is a wide, two-lane road with no shoulder. Since this section of road is near an interchange with I-89, it tends to have more traffic than other sections of the route. However, road visibility is good and the speed limit is low in the center of Hopkinton. The terrain is generally flat.

4.7 From The Cracker Barrel, retrace your route for 1.1 miles to the junction of Jewett Road. Continue east on US 202/NH 9/NH 103 an additional 1.5 miles to an unmarked road on the left. Note Whittier Pond on your left just before the turn.

Here US 202/NH 9/NH 103 is wide with no shoulder and generally carries moderate traffic. Most of the way you can coast downhill.

7.3 By Whittier Pond, turn left and follow the unmarked road for 2.6 miles until it rejoins the main highway.

Narrow, with a good surface, no shoulder, and well-shaded, this side road offers you a gentle downhill run away from the rush of traffic.

9.9 At the junction with US 202/NH 9/NH 103, turn left and ride 1.2 miles to Dunbarton Road, which is also the entrance to St. Paul's School.

The numbered highway remains wide with no shoulder and moderate traffic. Here you can coast most of the first mile, but there is a short uphill grade just before your next turn.

11.1 At Dunbarton Road, turn right and ride .8 mile to Silk Farm Road, on your left.

St. Paul's School, a private, coeducational, secondary school, is situated on 1,800 acres of woods and open land. Its manicured grounds and attractive buildings entice you to stop for a rest, or at least a look.

Dunbarton Road has a smooth surface, no shoulder, and very light traffic. The terrain is nearly level.

11.9 At Silk Farm Road, turn left and ride another .8 mile, passing under I-89, where the bicycle path leads off to the right.

Audubon House, located on Silk Farm Road .2 mile beyond the entrance to the bicycle path, is open from 9 a.m. to 5 p.m., Monday through Friday. Headquarters of the New Hampshire Audubon Society, it features a gift shop, library, and two short nature paths.

Silk Farm Road is similar to Dunbarton Road.

12.7 Immediately beyond the I-89 underpass, turn right onto the paved bicycle path, which parallels the interstate highway for 1.4 miles.

The bicycle path offers an excellent eight-foot-wide surface and no motorized traffic.

14.1 You are back at your start at the other end of the bicycle path.

Lawns and village greens are often handy places to stop on a warm summer's day.

11

Lake Sunapee Loop

23.2 miles; challenging cycling
Rolling to very hilly terrain

With its pine-covered islands, twenty-nine miles of jagged coastline, and crystal water, Lake Sunapee epitomizes the beauty of this rugged part of the Granite State. Mount Sunapee, third highest peak in southern New Hampshire, rises steeply from its western shore and provides a precipitous backdrop to this popular summer resort area. Because it is a retreat for those who enjoy fishing, swimming, and boating, our trip around the lake is highly recommended for early fall or late spring, the between-season times when snow-lovers and water-lovers are shifting gears.

And speaking of gears, this trip offers an excellent opportunity to refine your gear-shifting technique and to test your hill climbing philosophy. With a number of long, steep grades to conquer, both mind and body face a challenge. It also provides an opportunity to pit your cycling ability against that of others, for this is the route of the popular Sunapee Bike Race, held annually during the last weekend in August and sponsored by the First Citizens National Bank of Newport. The large number of participants are divided into categories based on age: Juniors (eighteen years and under), Seniors (nineteen to twenty-nine), and Veterans (over thirty). Members of the U.S. Cycling Federation who are devoted to serious racing must circle the twenty-two-mile course as many as four times. Should the prospect of such intense competition turn you off, take the trip on a cool, mid-September day when you can ride the loop at your own leisurely pace.

Begin your trip at the ski area parking lot in Mount Sunapee State

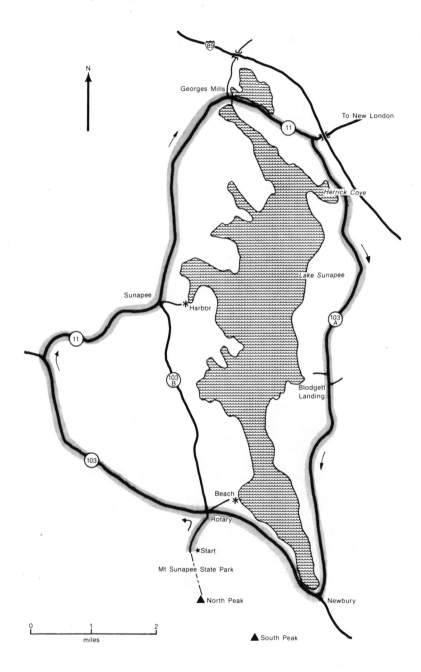

Park, located off NH 103 in Newbury. Simply follow the signs to the rotary by the park entrance and take the access road .7 mile uphill to its end by the base lodge.

0.0   From the parking lot, coast .7 mile back to NH 103, turn left, and head north on NH 103 for 4 miles to NH 11.

Mount Sunapee State Park offers a bit of something for everyone. For a nominal admission, you can swim at the park's sandy beach on Lake Sunapee, which can be reached from the well-marked access road off the rotary. A changing house is available, and a life guard is on duty during the summer months. Picnicking facilities, hiking trails, and a gondola to the top of Mount Sunapee are all located adjacent to the parking lot at the base of the ski slopes. During the first week in August the League of New Hampshire Craftsmen holds its annual fair here, and while this is a worthwhile event to attend, the unusually high volume of traffic

Spring, summer, and fall, the Lake Sunapee area attracts cyclists who seek ideal biking roads.

that it generates causes hazardous cycling conditions. Consequently, extreme caution is advised if you plan to cycle this route then.

A snack bar is located in both the base and summit lodges at the park. Perkins General Store is situated on the right just north of the Mount Sunapee rotary on NH 103.

NH 103 is a wide, two-lane road over rolling terrain with a smooth surface and paved shoulder suitable for biking. It offers excellent visibility and generally light to moderate traffic; during peak summer weekend hours the highway can be very busy, however.

4.7 At the junction of NH 103 and NH 11, turn right onto NH 11 and ride for 7.6 miles to NH 103A, just before the I-89 underpass. Note the sign for Newbury and Blodgett Landing.

Sunapee Harbor just off the main route makes a pleasant rest stop. Turn right at the blinking yellow light on NH 11, 2.5 miles beyond NH 103, and ride .5 mile to the water's edge. Should you wish an even closer look at the lake, the *M.V. Mount Sunapee* offers cruises daily at 10:30 a.m. and 2:30 p.m. from June 27 to Labor Day (603-763-5430). The *Sunapee Belle* offers a dockside lunch from noon to 1:30 p.m. and dining cruises on the lake at 5:45 p.m. and 7:45 p.m., also from June 27 to Labor Day (603-763-5477).

Several snackbars and restaurants are located near Sunapee Harbor. Gardners General Store, on NH 11 in Georges Mills .5 mile before the junction with NH 103A, is the last place to buy food until you reach Newbury.

Like NH 103, NH 11 is a wide two-lane highway with a smooth surface, paved shoulder, and light to moderate traffic conditions along much of the way. The terrain however is much more hilly, and there is one long steep hill just beyond the turn to Sunapee Harbor. Two miles beyond the same turn, the shoulders become intermittent and often unridable.

12.3 Following the sign to Blodgett Landing and Newbury, turn right and proceed south on NH 103A for 7.9 miles to its junction with NH 103 in Newbury.

Watch for the historical marker .8 mile south on NH 103A. During the golden age of steamboating on Lake Sunapee, the *Kearsarge, Ascutney, Armenia White,* and others brought hundreds of passengers to this location on Herrick Cove. From here they were transported by stage to New London's hotels and boarding houses. A lovely stone barn is situated on the right 6.2 miles from the junction of NH 11.

A general store and snack bar are located in Newbury at the junction of NH 103 and NH 103A.

NH 103A is narrow, with no shoulder but a smooth surface. While it carries less traffic than NH 103 and NH 11, it does have the steepest hills on the trip. However, because of the hills, the countryside is scenic and numerous old summer homes complement the landscape.

20.2 At the junction in Newbury, turn right and ride 2.3 miles to the Mount Sunapee rotary.

NH 103 from Newbury to the rotary is rolling and wide with a smooth surface and a paved shoulder.

22.5 At the rotary, turn left and climb .7 mile back uphill to the parking lot and your car.

23.2 Your tour ends here at the base of Mount Sunapee.

12

New London Lakes: Two short tours

The distance, difficulty, and terrain are stated at the beginning of each trip's directions.

It is little wonder that New London has long been a focal point of recreational activity in the Dartmouth–Lake Sunapee Region, for this hilltop town is surrounded by lakes and commands an exceptional view of 2,937-foot Mount Kearsarge. Situated at the northern end of Lake Sunapee, its history as a resort dates back to earlier times, before the internal combustion engine, when trains, steamboats, and carriages would deliver summer vacationers from Boston to its inns and hotels. Its Main Street still has ties to the past with fine old colonials, several inviting inns, and the red brick and mortar buildings of Colby-Sawyer College. Today New London functions both as a residential community and a year-round recreational center. Within easy reach of three major ski areas, three state parks, and numerous lakes, it is an ideal place for a holiday.

New London also offers interesting possibilities for cyclists. We have chosen here to describe two short, half-day trips, so those who might wish to couple cycling with other activities can do so easily. Because they are short, they are particularly suitable for those new to cycle touring, and while New London's location on a hilltop means negotiating several steep hills on the final leg of both tours, the climbs should cause no traumatic after-effects. Those wanting a longer day of riding can easily combine the two trips in a figure-eight pattern or take the Lake Sunapee trip described previously (see tour 11). Perhaps the most enticing way to approach your holiday here is to combine cycling with an overnight stay at the New London Inn

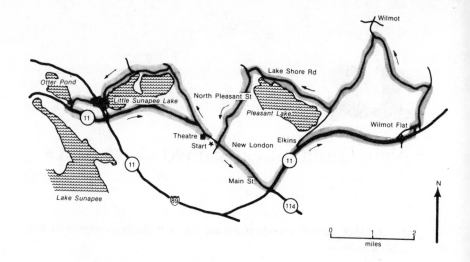

(603-526-2791), founded by Ezekiel Sargent in 1792, or at the Pleasant Lake Inn (603-526-6271), which was converted from a farm to an inn over one hundred years ago.

Both tours begin in the center of New London at the parking lot across from the Country Store Grocery and Kidder's Garage.

Little Sunapee Lake

10.5 miles; moderate cycling
Hilly terrain

0.0 From the parking lot, turn left onto Main Street and proceed for .5 mile, passing both the Edgewood Inn (no lodging offered) and the New London Barn Players Theater, to the blinking yellow light, where the road forks.

New London's Main Street has a variety of shops and well-kept old buildings.

There are several food stores in New London, including the Country Store Grocery and Cricenti's Market, where you can buy picnic food. New London also has a number of restaurants. Of special note is the Edgewood Inn, which, in addition to a health food store and craft shop, houses Peter Christian's Tavern, where you can select from an assortment of excellent homemade foods, including hearty soups, salads, sandwiches, and quiches. Note that the tavern is very busy during dinner hours.

Main Street is wide and level with moderate traffic and good visibility.

0.5 At the junction, continue straight on the right fork to Little Sunapee Lake.

The road toward Little Sunapee Lake offers views of the surrounding countryside before it actually descends to the lakeshore. Bucklin Beach, which you reach about 1 mile from the fork, offers fine swimming during the summer.

The route to Little Sunapee Lake is a narrow, twisting, two-lane road with a smooth surface and generally light traffic over hilly terrain.

2.1 At the sharp curve just beyond Bucklin Beach, bear left along the lakeshore, following the signs to Springfield and Grantham.

3.8 When the road begins to ascend gradually while curving right, another sign for Springfield and Grantham comes into view. Here, turn left onto a small unmarked road and ride for 1.6 miles to Otterville Road.

From the junction with the unmarked road to NH 11, which Otterville Road intersects, you travel narrow, hilly backcountry roads with some frost heaves and limited visibility.

5.4 At Otterville Road, turn left and ride for 1.1 miles to NH 11.

Otter Pond near the junction of Otterville Road and NH 11 offers fine swimming from the picnic area.

6.5 At the intersection, turn left onto NH 11 and ride for .8 mile to the I-89 and NH 11 interchange and then 3.2 miles on Main Street back to the center of New London.

NH 11 is a wide, two-lane road with a smooth surface wide, paved shoulders, excellent visibility, and moderate traffic.

10.5 You are back at the start of this short trip.

Pleasant Lake

14.9 miles; moderate to challenging cycling
Hilly terrain

0.0 From the parking lot opposite the Country Store Grocery, turn right onto Main Street and cycle for 1.6 miles past the New London Inn and Colby–Sawyer College, both on your left, to the traffic light where Main Street intersects NH 11.

Colby–Sawyer College, founded in 1837, enrolls around seven hundred women and offers degree programs in liberal arts and medical technology. As you coast down to the intersection of Main Street and NH 11 a panoramic view of Mount Kearsarge and adjacent mountains unfolds, a prelude to what you see on the fantastic downgrade on the next stretch to Wilmot Flat.

In addition to stores and restaurants already mentioned, you pass on this tour the Grey House. At the junction of Main Street and NH 11, it offers everything from ice cream cones to a full-course dinner.

Main Street is wide with good visibility, moderate traffic, and an intermittent shoulder. Exercise caution on the steep downgrade just before the junction.

Part of the fun of touring in New Hampshire is encountering the unexpected—in this case a huge yard sale.

1.6   At the intersection, turn left onto NH 11 and ride downhill for 3.7 miles to the turnoff for Wilmot Flat.

The views of Kearsarge and surrounding mountains on this stretch are breath-taking.

NH 11 along this downhill section is a wide, two-lane road with good visibility and an excellent paved shoulder suitable for cycling.

5.3   At the turnoff, turn left and ride for .1 mile to a T-junction in Wilmot Flat.

The roads from Wilmot Flat back to New London are generally narrow, curvy, and hilly with poor visibility but very low traffic. They vary from a relatively smooth surface to bumpy with a fair number of frost heaves.

5.4   At the T-junction in Wilmot Flat, turn right and ride past the post office to another T-junction.

5.5   At this junction, turn left onto the road to Wilmot and proceed for 1 mile to a road on the left just beyond a narrow bridge.

6.5   Just beyond the narrow bridge, turn left and ride for 2 miles to a yield sign.

8.5   At the yield sign, turn left again and ride another 2 miles to Lake Shore Road.

10.5   At the junction, head right to cycle along the north shore of Pleasant Lake.

From the Pleasant Lake Inn, you are treated to a great view of the lake. A historical marker near the inn recalls the exploits of the Pleasant Street Pioneers.

If you continue straight instead of turning right onto Lake Shore Road, you come in .3 mile to a small store in Elkins.

13.2   At the junction with North Pleasant Road, bear left and ride the remaining miles back to the center of New London.

14.9   Your tour ends on Main Street in the center of New London.

13

Canaan–Newfound Lake

54.5 miles; challenging cycling
Rolling to hilly terrain

Here is a trip for those who are primarily interested in a full day of rugged cycling. Bounded by the towns of Plymouth, Franklin, and Enfield, the rural area this tour circles through has until recently been forgotten by the tourists and developers attracted to the more glamorous Seacoast, Lakes, and White Mountain regions. It was perhaps the best-kept secret around, but people are now beginning to discover its clear lakes, rushing streams, and formidable mountains. While growth extending east from Hanover and west from Plymouth and Franklin may change the face of this part of New Hampshire in years to come, it is, for the immediate future at least, an excellent place to enjoy long distance rural cycling. Suggested for the more experienced cyclist, the ride offers long stretches where you can find a quiet unity of man and machine and relish the pace and rhythm of uninterrupted movement. With the exception of the stretch along the western shore of Newfound Lake, you should encounter little traffic. Unlike most of our other tours, this one does not offer numerous historic or architectural points of interest. Its beauty is to be found in waterfalls, sculptured rocks, and the other natural phenomena in which man has played little part.

Begin the trip in Canaan at the junction of US 4 and NH 118 near the east end of the main street. Parking should present no problem.

0.0   From the junction in Canaan, head north on NH 118 for 8 miles to paved River Road, on the right. This road is approximately .2 mile beyond the dirt crossroad that leads on the right to Province Road

State Forest. If you find yourself in the tiny village of Dorchester, you have continued too far on NH 118.

You come to the turnoff for Cardigan State Park approximately .5 mile north of Canaan on NH 118. While the park offers both picnicking and good hiking trails, we don't recommend that you make the detour unless you have plenty of time and energy. It is a 4-mile ride, sometimes uphill, into the park and another 4 miles back out, which would add considerably to an already long day. If you're bounding with energy, you may wish a shorter side trip to Cilley's Cave, where a hermit lived for nearly forty years. To get there, take the road to Cardigan State Park only as far as the town hall in Orange, park your bike, and then hike up the Orange Pond Trail, which starts behind the town hall.

The Canaan Country Store and George's Super Market are two places in Canaan where you can stock up on picnic food for your trip.

NH 118 is a two-lane road with an adequate biking surface and an unridable gravel shoulder. It is fairly level as you leave Canaan, but you do encounter some hills as you go farther north.

8.0 At River Road, turn right and proceed alongside the Baker River for 4.4 miles until you rejoin NH 118.

As you enjoy the pleasant downgrade along the Baker River's east side, keep an eye out for waterfalls and cascades.

River Road is smooth-surfaced with no traffic. While it is reasonably narrow it should present no cycling problems.

12.4 When you reach NH 118, turn right and ride for 1 mile to a four-way junction at the foot of a hill (approximately .5 mile beyond the Dorchester General Store).

The Dorchester General Store offers a snack bar, supplies, home-baked muffins, and outstanding hospitality. It is your last opportunity to buy food until you reach Hebron, eleven miles further on.

This stretch of NH 118 is similar to the one you were on earlier.

13.4 At the junction, turn sharply right to head towards Groton. The sign for Groton, on the right, is easy to miss, so watch carefully.

This road is a narrow, country byway with no shoulder, very little

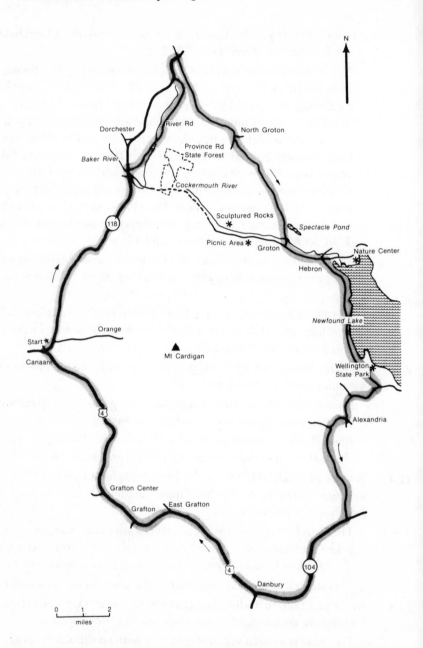

N

Dorchester
River Rd
North Groton
Province Rd
State Forest
Baker River
Cockermouth River
Sculptured Rocks
Spectacle Pond
Picnic Area
Groton
Nature Center
Hebron
(118)
Newfound Lake
Orange
Start
Mt Cardigan
Canaan
Wellington
State Park
(4)
Alexandria
Grafton Center
East Grafton
Grafton
(4)
(104)
Danbury

0   1   2
miles

traffic, and, part of the way, a rough surface. Over the first 1.9 miles you climb, sometimes steeply; then for the next 1.8 miles you descend through pleasant, open countryside.

17.1 At the bottom of the hill, at the fork, follow the main road as it heads to the right over a short bridge. There are signs here for Wellington State Park and Bristol, both of which are well beyond your next turn, which is 4.8 miles away in Groton.

The road continues as a narrow byway, but the surface improves. You climb again for .9 mile but are rewarded with a fantastic and often steep descent 3 miles long. The last .9 mile to Groton is fairly level.

21.9 At the intersection in Groton, turn sharply left to stay on the main road. Note another sign for Wellington State Park and Bristol pointing in your direction of travel. For 1.7 miles you ride through reasonably level valley farmland to the town of Hebron.

If you turn right at the intersection in Groton onto the minor road, you arrive at a picnic area by the Cockermouth River in 1.7 miles. Glaciers have sculptured potholes and rocks in the river that are great for sliding and swimming.

23.6 At the village green in Hebron, turn right onto West Shore Road, which you follow 5.6 miles along Newfound Lake to a stop sign.

Hebron is a pretty New Hampshire town with a schoolhouse, church, and general store fronting a gas-lit green. If instead of turning right you continue straight for approximately 1 mile, through Hebron, staying to the left of the green, you come to Paradise Point Audubon Nature Center at the northern end of Newfound Lake. It features natural history, environmental and wildlife exhibits, nature walks, and films. The Center is open daily from the last week in June through Labor Day between 10:00 a.m. and 5:00 p.m. A donation of $1 for adults and $.50 for children is requested. Wellington State Park, to your left on West Side Road 4.5 miles south of Hebron, is a welcome spot for hot, weary cyclists. The park offers swimming in Newfound Lake and picnicking facilities.

If you've depleted your food supplies, you can replenish them at the general store in Hebron.

West Shore Road is a narrow, two-lane road over rolling to hilly terrain with limited visibility. In summer, caution is urged because of heavy traffic. However, because the speed limit is only twenty and thirty miles per hour along this stretch, it can generally be cycled safely.

29.2   At the stop sign, turn right towards Alexandria and follow the main road 1.2 miles.

From West Shore Road to Alexandria and on to NH 104, the roads tend to be typical of backcountry New Hampshire: poor to fair surface, no shoulders, winding, and rolling.

The rivers and streams in the secluded region north of Canaan have carved potholes and wading pools.

30.4   Turn sharply left by the sign for Alexandria and ride .9 mile into the village. Stay with the main road as it turns right to head out of the village and then bends left to a fork.

31.4   At the fork, bear left onto the road marked for Danbury and ride 3.5 miles to NH 104.

34.9   When you reach NH 104, turn right and ride 5.5 miles to US 4 and the center of Danbury.

> NH 104 is a wide road with paved shoulders for 2.5 miles, good visibility, and fast traffic. The remaining 3 miles offer a good surface, but the shoulder turns to gravel and the roadway tends to be curvy.

40.4   In Danbury, turn right onto US 4 and bike for 14.1 miles through the Graftons back to Canaan.

> Because US 4 is fairly open, you have good views of the countryside and mountains along this stretch. The road to the Ruggles Mine, an old mine worth visiting, leaves from Grafton Center (there's a sign to direct you). However, we suggest you do not attempt the difficult ride up the steep grades on your bicycle. The road is very narrow and poorly surfaced, and the side trip is better made by automobile.

> Dick's General Store in Danbury is located on the left of NH 104 by the US 4 junction.

> US 4 is level to rolling, with good visibility, a smooth surface, and a gravel shoulder. While it is considered a major route, traffic is usually light due to the presence of I-89 just to the south.

54.5   You are in Canaan, your starting point.

14

Hanover–Orford

36.6 miles; moderate cycling
Rolling terrain

Hanover is the cultural and educational center of northwestern New Hampshire. Home of Dartmouth College, the Hopkins Center for the Performing Arts, and Mary Hitchcock Medical Center, it is a beehive of activity. Well-kept old college buildings, wide lawns bordering tree-lined streets, and the Hanover Inn overlooking an expansive village green lend a feeling of tradition and stability to the town. At the same time book-laden college students bustling between classes and the presence of numerous speciality shops catering to a diversity of interests and needs convey a sense of excitement and dynamism.

Yet, within five minutes of leaving town on this tour you are cycling amidst the farms, pastures, and corn fields of the northern Connecticut River Valley. While such a contrast results in momentary culture shock, the transition is a pleasant one to which you happily adapt. The cycling is generally easy, and the scenery often magnificent. The tour is classified as a moderate trip primarily because of its length, and we suggest you make it an all-day affair, allotting ample time for exploring the towns of Lyme and Orford. Also budget time for a picnic lunch along the bank of the Connecticut River, which you follow on your return from Orford. Slowly snaking its way between the round-topped hills of eastern Vermont and the foothills of New Hampshire's White Mountains, its serenity is contagious. With any luck at all, you'll return to Hanover relaxed, refreshed, and ready for a good dinner to end a perfect day.

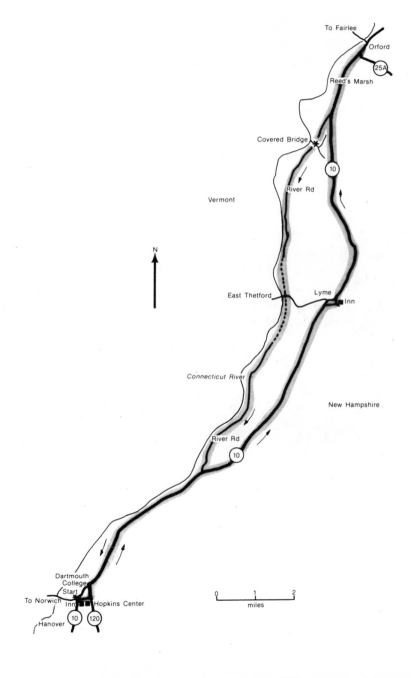

This trip begins by the Hanover Inn near the Dartmouth College green. While there are parking spaces available here, they are usually full, so you may want to head for nearby side streets or municipal lots.

0.0   From the green, follow East Wheelock Street, which is also NH 10, past the Hanover Inn and the Hopkins Center a couple of blocks to a traffic light. To stay on NH 10, turn left here and then right at the

Within minutes of leaving Hanover, you are cycling amidst pastoral scenes such as this one.

next traffic light. Continue north on NH 10 for 10.7 miles to Lyme. Dartmouth College, the Hopkins Center, and the town of Hanover offer a variety of activities too numerous to list here. For up-to-date information, call the Hopkins Center at 603-646-2422.

You can pick up your food supplies at one of several supermarkets on Hanover's main street (off NH 10 by the Hanover Inn) or at Pat and Tony's General Store, on the right on NH 10 approximately .5 mile north of the second traffic light. There are also several restaurants in Hanover.

NH 10 is a wide, smooth road with excellent shoulders. While traffic tends to be considerable in town, it thins out as you head north. The wide, paved shoulders provide ample room for cycling outside the traffic lanes. The terrain is hilly, but the roadway is well graded, resulting in more gradual slopes than might be expected. Visibility is excellent, and there are numerous expansive views of the Connecticut River and mountains and farms in both New Hampshire and Vermont.

10.7 In Lyme, bear sharply right off NH 10 onto the road that edges the right side of the long town common. At the head of the common turn left, in front of the Lyme Inn, and take the road between the church and horse sheds to a yield sign, where you rejoin NH 10. Continue north another 7.3 miles to Orford.

Lyme's Congregational Church was built in 1812 and its horse sheds are a rare example of original meeting house outbuildings. The Lyme Inn, built between 1802 and 1809, is a small, intimate country inn where area literati and artists often gather on Sunday afternoons for readings and discussions.

In Lyme you can purchase lunch or a snack at the counter in Nichol's Hardware or provisions at the Lyme Country Store, both facing the common on NH 10.

After you leave Lyme, NH 10 narrows and the shoulder, when it exists at all, is loose gravel. However, visibility remains excellent, and there are fewer hills. While traffic is generally light to moderate, it is also fast moving; we urge you to be careful.

18.0 At the red brick church in Orford, turn around and retrace your route 3.2 miles to a fork where there's a sign for Wilder Campground.

In Orford, you should note the seven "ridge" houses: built between 1773 and 1839, they display the influence of architects Charles Bulfinch and Asher Benjamin. Orford was also the home of Samuel Morey, who was credited with the invention of America's first marine steam engine, predating Robert Fulton's 1803 boat by nearly ten years.

Supplies can be purchased at the Elm Corner Market or the Orford General Store, both in Orford. You pass no more restaurants or stores until you return to the outskirts of Hanover.

21.2 At the fork, bear right off NH 10 and ride for 5.3 miles, through the Lyme–Edgell covered bridge, to a stop sign.

Reed's Marsh, a New Hampshire wildlife management area located just south of Orford and adjacent to the Connecticut River, supports a variety of bird, animal, and fish species. The Lyme–Edgell covered bridge, constructed in 1885 by Walter and J.C. Piper, is 154 feet long and crosses Clay Brook. The countryside around this backroad is mostly corn fields and pastureland. A way unlikely to be discovered by the passing tourist, it is always close to the river and affords some great views.

Although the backroads along the river are often cracked and bumpy, they are quite ridable. They are narrow with no shoulders, but have very little traffic. Note that 3.8 miles after you turn off NH 10 the road turns to gravel for 1 mile. However, it is hard-packed, wide, and level, so it should present no problem.

26.5 At the stop sign and crossroad that leads to the right, over the river, to Vermont, continue straight another 5.4 miles before rejoining NH 10.

The first 1.2 miles of this stretch are also hard-packed gravel, except for two short stony sections, where we advise you to walk your bike.

31.9 Turn right onto NH 10 and retrace the rest of your route for 4.7 miles back to Hanover.

36.6 You are back at your starting point in front of the Hanover Inn.

Seacoast and Lakes Regions

(17)

(16)

(15)

15

Exeter

28.5 miles; easy cycling
Level to rolling terrain

Here, cycling across the gently rolling terrain of New Hampshire's coastal plain, you are free to absorb the vistas that unfold before you, for there are few hills and little traffic to distract you on this route. A curve in the road may bring into view a tiny hamlet, an open expanse of pastureland, country-suburban residences, or the campus of one of America's most respected academies. Never strictly rural in nature, this trip begins in the bustling town of Exeter not far from the buildings of famed Phillips Exeter Academy and then loops south through attractive countryside, dipping briefly into neighboring Massachusetts. It is hard to imagine that this region sits on the edge of a major urban complex, for although the deep woods and mountains that characterize so much of New Hampshire are missing, there is still much open farmland and newer homes are well spaced. Particularly appealing are the acres of apple orchards with row upon row of trees brightly colored with blossoms in late spring and heavily laden with fruit in fall. But whatever the season, the roads, towns, countryside, and terrain of this region combine to offer a pleasant day of easy riding.

Your trip starts at the foot of Front Street in the center of Exeter, by the town hall and bandstand. Parking is available here and in the municipal lot behind Kurtz Restaurant, to your left on Water Street. Look for the signs indicating US 101/NH 108.

0.0   From the bandstand, turn right onto Water Street and head in the direction of NH 108 North. Almost immediately you come to a traffic light. US 101/NH 108 bears off to the left; your route continues straight on US 101C/NH 88 toward Hampton.

Although Exeter's roots are firmly planted in its seventeenth-century past, its townsfolk have managed to accommodate the change brought about by twentieth-century demands while preserving many of the historical landmarks. Because the many famous men who have lived in this town left their mark, there are a number of significant historical sites to visit. If you have time to explore the town, pick up the booklet of walking tours printed by the Exeter Historical Society. Also highly recommended is a tour of Phillips Exeter Academy, whose impact on the community has been considerable since its founding in 1781. Many of its buildings are open to the public.

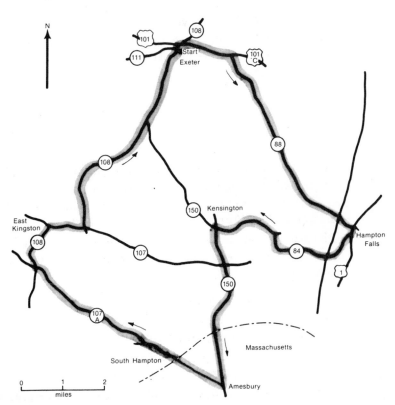

Grocery stores and restaurants abound in town. The Exeter Food Center, a grocery on Water Street just across from the Town Hall, is particularly convenient.

The route from Exeter to Hampton Falls is a winding country road along which houses are scattered. The surface is rather rough, but the roadway is level and bears little traffic.

1.3   At the fork where US 101C bears left to Hampton, bear right on NH 88 for 5.6 miles to a T-junction in Hampton Falls.

The 500-acre Applecrest Farm, 3.8 miles from Exeter, supports over twenty thousand apple trees, as well as smaller orchards of other fruit trees and some vegetable gardens. Fruit and produce, cider, maple syrup, home-baked breads and pastries, cheese and other items are sold at the farm's roadside store, Applecrest Apple-mart, on NH 88. In season you may pick your own fruit if you wish. As you come into Hampton Falls, note the quaint Unitarian Meeting House and then the Baptist Church, locally called the "Beer Bottle Church" because it is topped by a wooden copy of a beer bottle.

In addition to the goodies available at Applecrest Applemart, food is available at the R.P. Merrill and Son General Store in Hampton Falls.

6.9   At the junction in Hampton Falls, turn right onto US 1/NH 84 and then immediately right again onto the road signposted "Kensington." This is NH 84 (it is not so marked here), which you follow for 4.3 miles to NH 150 on the outskirts of Kensington.

NH 84 is a narrow, twisting, but level road. After taking you through a small residential area, it breaks into open countryside where there is little traffic.

11.2   At the junction, turn sharply left onto NH 150, continue straight across NH 107, and ride for 3.9 miles over the state line and into thickly settled Amesbury, Massachusetts.

If you want cold drinks, hot coffee, or snacks, watch for Pete's Variety on the right as you enter Amesbury.

NH 150 is wider than NH 84 and has gravel shoulders, good visibility, and light to moderate traffic. The terrain is more rolling than that over which you have just ridden.

15.1   In Amesbury watch carefully for your next turn, as there are no town signs or route numbers to give you warning. Just beyond Pete's Variety, on a slight downgrade by a triangular common, a sign reads, "Adventist Church—Welcome to Amesbury." At this point, make a very sharp right turn onto South Hampton Road, which becomes NH 107A as soon as it crosses the New Hampshire line. Continue on this road 6 miles, through South Hampton, to NH 108.

This stretch of NH 107A is a two-lane road with no shoulder, light traffic, and good visibility. There is one gradual climb to South Hampton, which is followed by a downgrade. The rest of the route is quite level.

There are few hills and surprisingly little traffic on the winding roads the Exeter tour follows.

21.1   At the junction, turn right onto NH 108 and ride 1.1 miles to the stop sign in East Kingston.

At the stop sign in East Kingston, Poggio General Store is in sight on your left.

NH 108 back to Exeter has a smooth surface, no shoulder, and moderate traffic. The terrain is level to rolling.

22.2   In East Kingston, turn right onto NH 107/NH 108 toward Exeter for .9 mile.

23.1   At the fork where NH 107 continues straight, bear left to stay on NH 108, which brings you back to Exeter in 5.4 miles.

28.5   At the yield sign in Exeter where NH 111 comes in from the left and US 101/NH 108 breaks off to the right, turn right onto Front Street to reach your point of departure.

16

Portsmouth–Little Boars Head

32.0 miles; easy cycling
Level to slightly rolling terrain

New Hampshire can lay claim to only a few miles of Atlantic coastline, but that short distance makes up in variety what it lacks in length. Here you find pounding surf, fine sandy beaches, and rocky cliffs; salt marshes and small harbors; old forts and old villages; and, in summer particularly, people. Because the sun and sea exert such a powerful attraction, you may encounter considerable traffic on this trip, especially on summer weekends. Consequently, we strongly suggest that you venture here only during midweek in summer or preferably in late spring or early fall, when there is ample warmth, solitude, and space for an exhilarating ride.

Cruise along the winding road that parallels the shoreline and enjoy the great expanses of ocean views. On clear days, the Isle of Shoals lighthouse is visible over ten miles offshore, and you can often see freighters or sailing boats on the horizon. In addition to providing recreation, the ocean is still an avenue of travel, just as it was when early settlers found their way in 1623 to this shore's safe harbors. Much of the region's early history is preserved in numerous historical sites along the route, the most notable of which is Portsmouth's Strawbery Banke. This trip also takes you inland a short way through open, level farmland with weathered homes and barns. It is an ideal outing for those who wish to couple easy cycling with a generous diversity of potential activities.

To reach the tour's start in the Strawbery Banke area of Portsmouth, follow the small strawberry signs posted along major routes into town. Parking is usually available on side streets around the

Banke, or in the municipal lot next to Prescott Park; the lot's entrance
is by the corner of Marcy and State streets, adjacent to the old draw-
bridge to Kittery, Maine.

0.0   From the parking lot, turn left onto Marcy Street and cycle .4 mile to
its end at a four-way intersection.

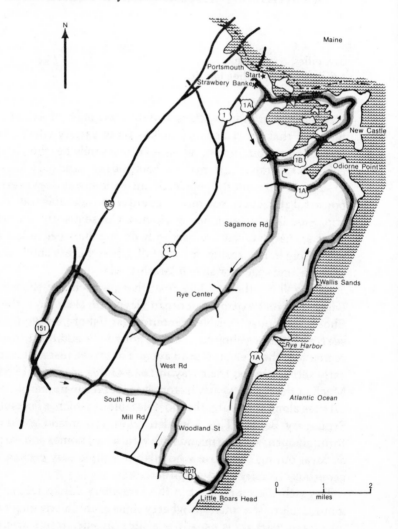

You pass the entrance to Strawbery Banke, a ten-acre museum that contains more than thirty buildings dating from the seventeenth, eighteenth, and nineteenth centuries. The grounds are open from May 1 to October 31. The lawns and gardens of Prescott Park, across the street from the Banke's entrance and stretching to the piers along the Piscataqua River, are the setting for an annual summer-long arts festival of plays and concerts, among other events.

There are many fine restaurants in the Strawbery Banke area of Portsmouth. Karen's Ice Cream Parlor, on State Street, offers homemade ice cream, among other goodies, and natural foods are available in the Hart House General Store, on Marcy Street just before the four-way intersection.

Marcy Street is an old narrow, winding city street.

0.4 At the intersection, continue straight on South Street, passing the Blue Fin fish market on the left and following the signs to Hampton and Rye. Continue straight through two blinking lights to a traffic light at the junction of US 1A.

You pass Marconi's Grocery, on the right, on South Street.

South Street is similar to Marcy, but slightly wider.

1.0 At the traffic light, turn left onto UA 1A, also called Sagamore Road, keeping the cemetery on your left. Continue on this road for 1.6 miles, passing the intersection where US 1B leads left toward New Castle, to a four-way intersection with a blinking light, where US 1A curves sharply left.

You pass the Bridge House Restaurant and the Grove Grocery by the US 1B intersection and Muffins Unlimited, a bakery, just before reaching the blinking light.

US 1A is a wide two-lane road through a residential section of Portsmouth. While there may be a substantial amount of traffic, the speed limit is low. You should ride as carefully here as you would in any city. Please note that the bridge just before the US 1B junction has open grates and should be walked over.

2.6 Where US 1A bears left towards Odiorne Point State Park, you continue straight on Sagamore Road toward Rye Center.

The roads you cycle between this junction and Little Boars Head,

You should walk across the open-grate bridge by Wentworth-by-the-Sea, but the view of Little Harbor and Odiorne Point more than compensates for any inconvenience.

where you pick up US 1A again, are narrow with fair surfaces, no shoulders, good visibility, and little traffic. The terrain is generally level.

3.6   Where Clark Road forks straight, curve right to stay on Sagamore Road.

4.1   At the next curve, bear right again on the road posted for Boston and Rye Center.

5.2   Just before you enter the center of Rye, your route merges with Washington Road. Bear right, on Washington Road, and pass the Rye School.

There is a Cumberland Farms grocery on the right where you join Washington Road.

5.6   In Rye Center, keep to the right of the war monument, following Washington Road toward Route 1, Boston, and Manchester.

Time seems to have stood still in this part of Rye. Salt marshes, woods, and gardens stretch away from the many huge old homes that line the road you follow. In the center of the village you can visit the burial ground from the Indian Massacre of 1691.

7.7   At the traffic light at the US 1 intersection, continue straight, following the road 1.7 miles to a stop sign just beyond the I-95 overpass.

9.4   At the stop sign, turn left onto NH 151 and cycle roughly parallel to the interstate for 2.5 miles, this time passing over the superhighway.

11.9   Just beyond the overpass, turn left onto the road marked for the Sagamore–Hampton Golf Course. Continue for .9 mile to a stop sign at the junction of US 1.

12.8   At the stop sign, turn left and then immediately right onto South Road. Cycle along this road 1.9 miles to Woodland Road.

14.7   At this corner, turn right onto Woodland Road and ride for 1.4 miles to the stop sign at the junction of US 101D (Atlantic Avenue).

16.1   At the junction, turn left and head toward Little Boars Head, 1.2 miles away.

17.3   When you reach US 1A (Ocean Boulevard) at Little Boars Head, turn left for the 9.6-mile ride along the seashore.

Along US 1A, you pass numerous seaside mansions with sweeping lawns and rose gardens and many smaller weathered structures with antique and craft shops. Rye Harbor State Park, a wayside park on a point of land jutting into the ocean and an ideal spot for a picnic, is located 4 miles beyond Little Boars Head. Wallis Sands State Park, 2.2 miles beyond Rye Harbor, is a well-known swimming and sunning spot, while Odiorne Point State Park, 1.6 miles north of Wallis Sands, offers picnicking and hiking trails. It is also the site of Fort Dearborn and an Audubon Center.

Along US 1A, there are numerous restaurants specializing in seafood and snack bars. In summer only, groceries are available by the Dunes Motel, 2.4 miles from Little Boars Head. Year-round they are available at Philbrick's Store, .2 mile further on, and at the Red Roof Supermarket, 3.4 miles further on.

US 1A along the Atlantic shoreline is narrow and winding with a minimal shoulder. Traffic here can be heavy, especially on summer weekends; so you should use extreme caution if you cycle then.

26.9   When you reach the blinking light at the four-way intersection through which you continued straight on your way to Rye Center, turn right to retrace your way on US 1A for .5 mile, as far as the US 1B cutoff to New Castle.

27.4   At the junction, turn right onto US 1B and follow this route 4.2 miles through New Castle back to Portsmouth.

On US 1B you pass Wentworth-by-the-Sea, one of the few New Hampshire resort hotels remaining in operation that retains the grandeur of the nineteenth century. The town of New Castle, an island village dating back to 1623, is worth exploring. Its winding, narrow streets, Great Island Common, and the ruins of Fort Constitution combine to provide constant interest.

Food is available at the Great Island Store on US 1B in the center of New Castle.

US 1B is, like US 1A, narrow and winding, but it carries less traffic. Exercise caution at the cross-grid bridge just before Wentworth-by-the-Sea and at the two bridges that bring you from Newcastle to Portsmouth. These last two have paved roadways but open-grate shoulders.

31.6   When you come again to the four-way intersection in Portsmouth by the Blue Fin fish market, turn right to retrace your route up Marcy Street to your start.

32.0   You are back at Prescott Park, where you began the tour.

17

Tamworth–North Sandwich

23.1 miles; moderate cycling
Rolling to hilly terrain, some short steep hills

Between the White Mountain National Forest in the north and Lake Winnipesaukee in the south, this area is surprisingly free of commercial recreational services and development. For the cyclist, this is a rather happy circumstance. Not unlike a quiet child who is often overshadowed by the obvious exploits of an older sibling, it is a section of New Hampshire whose charm and beauty becomes apparent only upon close examination. Let the masses hike the mountains and swim in the lakes; leave the little country roads in Tamworth, Wonalancet, and North Sandwich the domain of the cyclist.

Passing through a mixture of farms, forests, and one-store towns, this is a good trip for someone who seeks a respite from the rush of urban life or the pressures of a demanding job. Because the area is not overrun with numerous activities to entice you off your bike, you should be content to negotiate the twists and turns and ups and downs of backcountry roads. And while the tour covers enough distance and hills to make you know you have been cycling, it is also a trip that should not leave you exhausted and spent.

Your tour begins on the main street of Tamworth, near the junction of NH 113 and NH 113A. You should have no problem finding parking.

0.0 From the center of Tamworth, cycle back to the junction of NH 113 and NH 113A.

The Barnstormers Playhouse, located at the west end of Tamworth's main street, houses a summer theater group that is the oldest in New Hampshire and one of the oldest in the United States. It was founded by Francis Grover Cleveland, son of our twenty-second president, in 1931. While the players once did an eighty-mile weekly circuit, they now perform only at their Tamworth home.

Remick's Grocery in Tamworth is the only place to buy food until you reach North Sandwich, approximately fourteen miles into your trip.

0.1   At the junction of numbered highways, turn left onto NH 113A, heading towards Wonalancet.

NH 113A, the Chinook Trail, is a very windy, roller-coaster road with a rough surface and no shoulder. Visibility is generally poor due to frequent dips and curves, but because traffic tends to be light, this should not present a major problem.

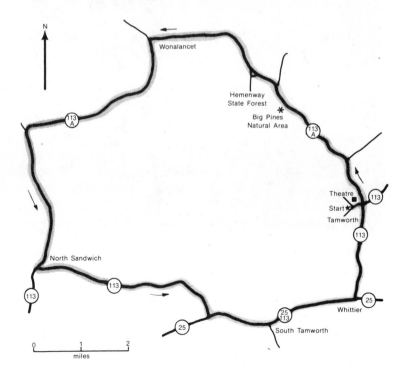

Mountain vistas are just some of the many treats on the Tamworth–North Sandwich tour.

1.1   When the road forks, stay left and head up a short hill. This fork is well marked with signs for Wonalancet, Sandwich, and NH 113A, all pointing in the direction you are going. Continue on this winding road for 5.6 miles to Wonalancet.

Big Pines Natural Area, part of Hemenway State Forest, is located on the left, 1.8 miles north of the fork. Its cool, shady woods are inviting on a hot day.

6.7   In Wonalancet, NH 113A turns sharply left. Turn left and follow it for 6.9 miles to NH 113 in North Sandwich.

The countryside is very pleasant with rolling farmland, stone fences, and stands of birch and pine through which you get occasional glimpses of the nearby mountains.

This stretch of NH 113A is similar to the one you just traveled: traffic is light, but visibility is poor and there is no shoulder.

13.6 In North Sandwich, turn left onto NH 113 and ride for 3.9 miles to the junction with NH 25.

In North Sandwich food supplies are available at Ye Olde Country Store; instead of turning left at the junction of NH 113A and NH 113, continue straight for .2 mile to the village proper. The store is on the right.

Road conditions on NH 113 are similar to those on NH 113A.

17.5 At the intersection with NH 25, turn left onto NH 25/NH 113 and ride for 3.2 miles along the Bearcamp River through South Tamworth to Whittier. The numbered highways split in Whittier just beyond the Whittier Cash Market.

The Mountain Villa Restaurant is located in Whittier .5 mile after NH 25 and NH 113 divide. Food can also be purchased at the Whittier Cash Market.

NH 25 is a primary New Hampshire route. This section has a smooth surface and a fairly consistent three-foot-wide paved shoulder that occasionally disappears when the road crosses a narrow bridge. Traffic tends to be moderate and steady. Because it is quite level, offers good visibility, and has a ridable shoulder, it is a reasonably safe road to cycle, despite the traffic.

20.7 At the fork in Whittier, bear left onto NH 113 and proceed for 2.3 miles back to the road to Tamworth village.

23.0 At the junction of NH 113 and NH 113A, turn left onto the main street of Tamworth.

23.1 You are back at your start.

North Country

18

North Conway–Bear Notch

38.7 miles; moderate to challenging cycling
Level to rolling terrain, many downgrades and one long, gradual climb

North Conway, the starting point for this trip, is a year-round resort community located on US 302/NH 16 at the southeastern edge of the White Mountain National Forest. As the major gateway to the Presidential Range, it offers a wide variety of services to the tourist and outdoorman, including numerous specialty shops, restaurants, and overnight accommodations. Because thousands of people disperse from this town each year to the White Mountains, it is difficult to develop a trip here that avoids high traffic conditions at least part of the way. Coupled with the traffic problem is that of extremely long upgrades, which can make cycling a punishment rather than a pleasure, especially for the weekend cyclist. Nonetheless, our North Conway–Bear Notch trip offers an excellent opportunity to see by bicycle a particularly beautiful section of New Hampshire. The route we have chosen involves only one long, gradual climb, through Bear Notch. The rest of the way winds along the Saco and Swift rivers through level to rolling terrain and includes lots of gentle downgrades to make cycling exhilerating and effortless. To put the icing on the cake, the road conditions are quite good, the traffic generally light, and the scenery spectacular.

Your route begins at the north end of North Conway, near the Eastern Mountain Sports shop (the old Eastern Slopes Inn), where there is unmetered on-street parking.

0.0   Head north on US 302/NH 16 a very short distance to River Road, on the left by the Gulf station and just beyond the Eastern Mountain Sports store.

The many shops, restaurants, overnight accommodations, and tourist attractions in the Conway–North Conway area are too numerous to mention. A stop at one of the tourist information centers will provide all the brochures about the area you may need.

North Conway's main thoroughfare is lined with restaurants and food shops.

US 302/NH 16 within North Conway is a busy road where traffic is often heavy but slow moving.

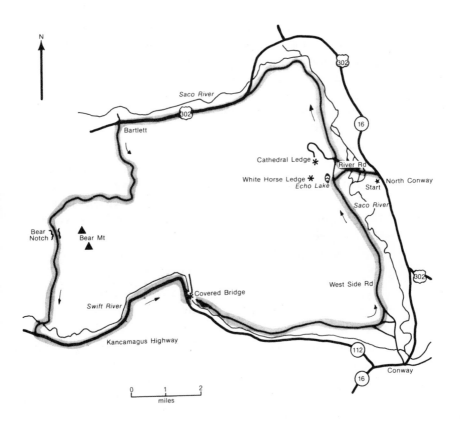

0.1   At the intersection, turn left onto River Road, riding downhill under the railroad bridge toward the Saco River, which you cross in 1 mile.

River Road tends to be narrow with no shoulder.

1.1   Immediately after crossing the Saco River, your road merges with West Side Road, which comes in from the left. Continue straight on this road for another 5.6 miles to US 302.

At the junction with West Side Road you can see clearly White Horse and Cathedral ledges, two rock cliffs rising abruptly from the valley floor. In .5 mile you pass a paved access road to Cathedral Ledge; the climb to the top is tough for cyclists, but the view from there is outstanding. Foot trails also provide an easy hike to the top. Diana's Baths, a popular natural area with smooth rocks and refreshing pools, can be reached by trail from West Side Road approximately 1 mile beyond the turnoff for Cathedral Ledge. A historical marker commemorating Lady Blanche, a noted writer and contributor to *Harper's* and the *Atlantic Monthly* who lived in a nearby cottage, is located on the right .7 mile beyond the trail to Diana's Baths.

There are few stores on West Side Road.

This stretch of road also tends to be narrow with no shoulder. The visibility is generally good although there are sections where the road curves and rolls enough to restrict your vision. Traffic patterns are difficult to predict in this area, but this road is certainly less traveled than US 302/NH 16.

6.7   At the intersection with US 302, turn left and ride for 4.1 miles to the blinking light in Bartlett just beyond the Bartlett Hotel.

There are several restaurants and a few food stores along the section of US 302 you travel and in the village of Bartlett.

US 302 is a wide, two-lane road with a smooth surface, and intermittent shoulder, and excellent visibility. Because it is one of the three major roads through the White Mountains, it often carries moderate to heavy traffic traveling at highway speeds. Because of its width and good visibility it can be ridden safely by the competent cyclist. Caution is urged, however.

10.8   From the blinking light in Bartlett, turn left onto Bear Notch Road.

There are several turnoffs along Bear Notch Road that offer excellent views of the Presidential Range.

Bear Notch Road is a forest highway with light traffic. It is wide, has good visibility, and has been nicely graded to provide a smooth gradual rise over the 4.1-mile ascent to Bear Notch. Once over the crest, you have a 4.4-mile downgrade to NH 112, the Kancamagus Highway.

19.3 At the intersection, turn left onto the Kancamagus Highway, and ride 6.1 miles to the covered bridge at Blackberry Crossing.

Be sure to stop at the Rocky Gorge Scenic Area, on the left 3.5 miles beyond the junction of Bear Notch Road, and at Lower Falls Scenic

The Albany Bridge leads you off the Kancamagus Highway onto a lightly traveled back road.

Area, also on the left 2 miles beyond Rocky Gorge. Both offer opportunities to swim in the clear, rushing waters of the Swift River and to picnic by the waterfalls.

The Kancamagus Highway has an even better surface than Bear Notch Road but carries much more traffic, especially on weekends. Although visibility is excellent and traffic tends to travel at low speeds, we urge you to use caution here.

25.4   At Blackberry Crossing, turn left and immediately cross the Swift River through a covered bridge. Take an immediate right on the far side of the bridge and ride for 6.6 miles to West Side Road; there is no sign posted here.

The Albany covered bridge was built in 1859.

From Blackberry Crossing to West Side Road, the road is a narrow, country byway with some frost heaves, no shoulder, and lots of dips, rises, and curves. While visibility is restricted and road conditions are poor, traffic tends to be very light.

32.0   At the junction by West Side Road, turn left and cycle 5.6 miles back to River Road by the Saco River.

About .5 mile before you reach River Road you pass Echo Lake State Park, which offers picnicking, hiking, and swimming.

There is one restaurant on this section of West Side Road.

West Side Road is quite level and provides for easy cycling. It is smooth but lacks a shoulder. Traffic is usually light to moderate.

37.6   At the junction with River Road, turn right and cycle back to US 302/NH 16 and your car.

38.7   You are back at your start by the Eastern Mountain Sports store in North Conway.

19

Sugar Hill

14.4 miles; moderate cycling
Level to rolling terrain, one long hill

Sugar Hill is a small, "undeveloped" resort town on the western slope of the White Mountains. Commanding exceptional views of the surrounding countryside, its name comes from a large grove of sugar maples found in the area. Having broken ties with the adjacent town of Lisbon in 1962, it is New Hampshire's youngest town.

We selected Sugar Hill as the focal point of this short trip because it couples scenic beauty with low traffic conditions and avoids the commercial development that characterizes many other tourist "meccas" in the White Mountains. Although you can easily complete the loop in a morning or afternoon, if you bring a picnic lunch and the weather invites swimming it can also be easily stretched out to a leisurely all-day affair. From a lazy cyclist's point of view, the only drawback is the long (nearly five miles) gradual climb to Sugar Hill, but that comes in the middle part of the tour after you have loosened up your bike legs. It also means that you can cap the tour with an equally long descent.

We suggest you start this trip in Lisbon, midway between the towns of Woodsville and Littleton on US 302/NH 10. Parking is available in and around the center of town.

0.0   From the junction of US 302/NH 10 and School Street in the center of town, head west on School Street, immediately crossing the Ammonoosuc River. Just beyond the bridge, by the Lisbon Town Hall, a large red Victorian frame structure, turn right onto Water Street/Lyman Road.

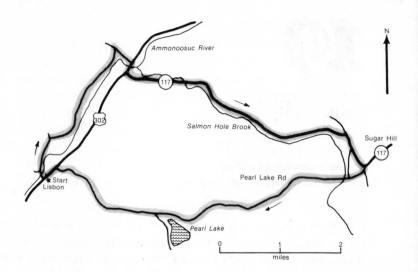

For more than three miles you parallel the Ammonoosuc River, which meanders through a narrow valley dotted with farm buildings and open fields.

If you plan to purchase food, stock up in Lisbon as there are no other stores along this tour.

The roads paralleling the Ammonoosuc are narrow with fairly rough but ridable surfaces over level to rolling terrain. While there is no shoulder, the traffic is very light.

0.8   Just beyond the New Hampshire Electrical Cooperative building, on the right, turn right onto an unmarked road and continue alongside the Ammonoosuc River for another 2 miles to a junction with another unmarked road.

2.8   At the junction, turn right onto the unmarked road and ride .5 mile to US 302/NH 10.

3.3   At the junction, turn right onto the numbered highway, cross another bridge over the Ammonoosuc, and immediately turn left onto NH 117. You cycle up this road for 4.9 miles to reach the village of Sugar Hill.

NH 117 follows Salmon Hole Brook, reputed at one time to have an inexhaustable supply of fish. Whether that reputation holds true today is doubtful, but fishless or not, the brook does offer occasional opportunities to cool off on a hot summer day.

NH 117 is wider than the roads you have just traveled and has a smooth surface. Its shoulder is of variable quality, however, and because it slopes away from the road it is not particularly enjoyable to ride. It does provide a place to go if necessary, though. While you are climbing steadily towards Sugar Hill on this stretch, road visibility and views of the surrounding countryside are excellent. Traffic tends to be light.

8.2 At the wood sign with white letters saying "Pearl Lake Road," turn sharply right and immediately begin a 6-mile-long descent back to Lisbon.

At this junction, NH 117 curves upward and to the left into the village of Sugar Hill. If you can handle one more short ascent, follow it past the Pearl Lake Road turnoff through the center of the village and then turn around. You pass many pleasant homes as well as the Sugar Hill Meeting House on the left, a structure built in 1830 and capped with a cupola and clock. The village also offers some spectacular views of the surrounding countryside, with the White Mountains as a backdrop.

The Homestead, built in 1802 and filled with a variety of antiques, and the Sugar Hill Inn, a 1750 farmhouse converted to an inn in 1925, are both excellent places to dine and spend the night, should you wish to couple cycling with a stay at a New Hampshire country inn.

Pearl Lake Road offers an exceptionally scenic ride past open fields, farms (including one with a granite barn), alongside a stream and through stands of pine and birch. Pearl Lake, on your left, is a gem with no development around it and no apparent restrictions on swimming.

Pearl Lake Road is narrow and bumpy with no shoulder, little traffic, some steep downgrades, and occasional sharp curves. Exercise caution on the downgrades, as it is easy here to get going too fast to negotiate some of the sharp curves safely.

14.2 At the fork 6 miles from Sugar Hill, bear right down a short steep hill

Stands of birch line Pearl Lake Road, your return route on the Sugar Hill tour.

and cross the railroad tracks to reach US 302/NH 10. Turn left and ride for .2 mile to your start.

US 302/NH 10 is a primary road with a smooth surface, moderate to heavy traffic, and very little shoulder. However, since you are within the Lisbon town limits, traffic tends to be slow for the short distance you must be on it.

14.4   You are back at your start by School Street.

20

Dixville Notch Century

105.7 miles; very challenging cycling (one-day tour) or moderate to challenging (two- or three-day tour) cycling
Level to rolling terrain, one long climb; then rolling to hilly terrain

A book on cycle touring would not be complete without a "Century ride" allowing the adventurous and experienced rider the opportunity to cover a hundred or more miles in one day. While New Hampshire's topographical extremes can make a Century a difficult goal to obtain, even for the experienced cyclist, our Dixville Notch trip offers a superb challenge to a wide segment of the cycling population, because those who aren't up to Century standards can easily convert this trip into a two- or three-day mini-vacation using either campsites or motels along the way.

With a mountain to cross and a number of hills to climb, especially in the trip's second half, the difficulty of this tour should not be underestimated. Much of the terrain, however, is level to gently rolling through some of the most beautiful and remote sections of New Hampshire. If you elect to take it you should be well equipped, have reasonable knowledge of bike maintenance, and carry a good tool kit, some spare parts, and emergency provisions in case you get stuck for the night.

This is not a trip that offers numerous alternate activities to complement your day of riding. You should love to ride and you should be able to appreciate the wonders of northern New Hampshire's wilderness: the Androscoggin River, Dixville Notch with its sheer cliffs edged by pines and white birches, and the Connecticut River while it is still a narrow, meandering stream. Probably one of the most appealing aspects of the trip is the openness of the terrain. Often in New Hampshire your view is restricted by heavy growth near the roadway; our Dixville Notch trip, however, tends to provide long, sweeping views of the north country.

Begin your trip at the municipal parking lot near the City Hall in Berlin. To get there, take NH 16 North, passing the Berlin City Bank on your left, to the traffic light by City Hall and a B.P. gas station, to your right. Turn right at this light and go over a bridge. Before you reach a second bridge, you come to a free municipal parking lot. If you plan to make this more than a one-day trip, we suggest you notify the Berlin Police that you are leaving your car overnight.

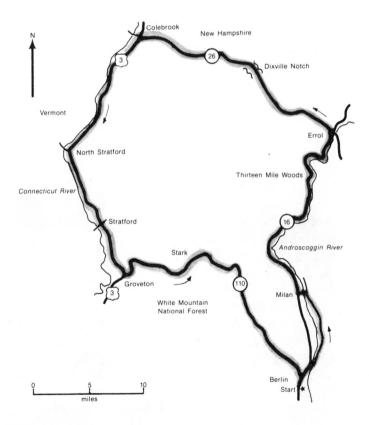

0.0   From the parking lot, retrace your route to NH 16 by City Hall, turn right onto NH 16 and ride for 1.7 miles to a traffic light just beyond Rotary Park.

There are numerous food stores and restaurants in Berlin and we strongly urge you to stock up before you leave town. Once you are north of this city, there are very few stores of any kind until Errol, and even these services are minimal.

NH 16 from City Hall to the traffic light by Rotary Park offers poor riding conditions through heavy traffic.

1.7   At the light, turn right, crossing a new steel bridge, and immediately bear left, heading north along the east bank of the Androscoggin River for 6.7 miles to Milan.

The road on this side of the river generally has a smooth surface, little traffic, fair visibility, and no shoulder. The terrain you pass through is level.

Although the Dixville Notch tour can be ridden as a Century, it passes through some lovely camping countryside.

8.4   By the sign for NH 16 in Milan, turn left and cycle .4 mile, crossing the Androscoggin again, to NH 16.

8.8   At the junction with NH 16, turn right. You cycle north on NH 16 for 21.6 miles to Errol.

While this entire section of the trip is wild and beautiful, Thirteen Mile Woods Scenic Area is particularly outstanding. Managed by the Seven Islands Land Company, the Brown Company, and the State of New Hampshire, there is no development of any kind along this stretch of road, which closely parallels the west bank of the Androscoggin and offers many places to stop and enjoy the solitude of wilderness. The Androscoggin State Wayside Area 16.8 miles north of Milan has picnic tables and basic toilet facilities. The Androscoggin itself is a well-known and very popular river for canoeing.

Camping is allowed by permit only along this section and only in one designated area, Mollidgewock Campground, 19.2 miles north of Milan. For information about the campground, permits, and canoeing on the Androscoggin, call 603-486-7770.

From Milan to Errol, NH 16 has a smooth surface, little or no shoulder, excellent visibility, and, normally, light traffic. The terrain here is flat to gently rolling.

30.4   In Errol, turn left onto NH 26 for the 22.3-mile ride through Dixville Notch to the junction of US 3 in Colebrook.

With birch and fir trees growing out of sheer rock walls, Dixville Notch makes this climb worth the effort, especially after you cross the top. You are immediately rewarded with a view of the Balsams, a luxury resort often referred to as America's Switzerland because of its setting, architecture, and atmosphere.

Accommodations along this stretch of the route are available at Log Haven Cabins and Camping Area, 7 miles west of Errol on NH 26, at the Balsams, 4 miles further on, and at the Redwood Motel 6 miles east of Colebrook.

Food is available at both the Errol and Umbagog restaurants on NH 26 in Errol and at the Errol General Store, to the right on NH 26. Closer to Colebrook is the Redwood Restaurant.

NH 26 is a wide road with a smooth surface, good visibility, little traffic, and generally very little shoulder. However, because it is a primary highway, traffic tends to move fast. The terrain here is generally level to rolling through forest and farm country; the only significant climb is 1.7 miles long up to Dixville Notch. West of the notch there is a long, sinuous downgrade.

52.7   In Colebrook, turn left onto US 3 and ride for 26.9 miles along the Connecticut River to Groveton.

This route along the east side of the Connecticut River offers many good views of the river and adjacent Vermont. Note the historical marker 14.8 miles south of Colebrook recounting early log drives down the river. Just before you reach your turnoff in Groveton, you pass a covered bridge.

Several motels along US 3 in Colebrook offer accommodations. Colebrook and North Stratford both have restaurants and food stores.

US 3 is the major road linking the southern half of the state with Canada. Consequently, it carries some fast traffic and many trucks. It is also the most hilly road on this route, with fairly consistent ups and downs. However, the road is quite wide, the surface smooth, and the visibility good. For the most part, there is no shoulder.

79.6   In Groveton, turn left onto NH 110 and ride 26.1 miles back to Berlin.

The village of Stark, 7 miles east of Groveton on NH 110 offers one of the most widely photographed New Hampshire scenes: the Stark covered bridge and adjacent church, both set against a backdrop of sheer cliffs.

Accommodations are available at several motels in Groveton and at the Millbrook Inn and Campground adjacent to NH 110 in Stark.

NH 110 offers a wide, smooth surface with a consistent paved shoulder. There are some long ascents and descents; however, they tend to be more gradual than those on US 3. Road visibility is excellent, traffic tends to be light, and the views are great. As you approach Berlin, though, the shoulder disappears, the traffic increases, and riding conditions become distinctly urban. The last stretch of NH 110 takes you through a heavy commercial and industrial area.

104.6 At the traffic light by Collier's General Store, on the left, a sign points left towards NH 16. Turn left and ride one block to Madigan Street. Here, turn right and ride one block, and then bear left by Ron's Meat Market. Continue downhill past the Berlin Police Station and through the railroad underpass to the traffic light by Dunkin' Donuts. Turn right, cycle one block, and then turn left onto NH 16. Continue past the Berlin City Bank to the traffic light by City Hall, where you turn right.

105.7 You are back at the parking lot where your trip began.

Guidebooks from New Hampshire Publishing Company

Written for people of all ages and experience, these highly popular and carefully prepared books feature detailed directions, notes on points of interest, sketch maps, and photographs.

For bicyclists—

20 Bicycle Tours in Vermont, by John S. Freidin. $5.95
20 Bicycle Tours in New Hampshire, by Tom and Susan Heavey. $5.95

About New Hampshire—

25 Ski Tours in the White Mountains, by Sally and Daniel Ford. $4.95
Fifty Hikes in the White Mountains, by Daniel Doan. $6.95
Fifty More Hikes in the White Mountains, by Daniel Doan. $6.95
25 Walks in the Dartmouth-Lake Sunapee Region, by Mary L. Kibling. $4.95
25 Walks in the Lakes Region, by Paul H. Blaisdell. $4.95
Canoe Camping Vermont and New Hampshire Rivers, by Roioli Schweiker. $4.95
A Year with New England's Birds: A Guide to Twenty-five Field Trips, by Sandy Mallett. $5.95
Country Northward: A Hiker's Journal on the Trail in the White Mountains of New Hampshire, by Daniel Ford. $6.95

Available from bookstores, sporting goods stores, or the publisher. For a complete description of these and other guides in the *Fifty Hikes, 25 Walks,* and *25 Ski Tours* series, write: New Hampshire Publishing Co., Box 70, Somersworth, NH 03878.